Grub on a Grant

GRUB
ON A GRANT

Cas Clarke

Illustrations by
Mike Gordon

HEADLINE

Copyright © text 1985, 1986, 1991 Cas Clarke
Copyright © illustrations 1985, 1991 Mike Gordon

First published in Great Britain in 1985 by
Columbus Books Limited
Revised and expanded edition published in 1988

Reprinted 1989
by Virgin Books, a division of W.H. Allen & Co plc

Reprinted 1990
by HEADLINE BOOK PUBLISHING PLC

Expanded edition published in 1991
by HEADLINE BOOK PUBLISHING PLC

Designed by Pat Craddock

ISBN 0 7472 3560 0

Printed and bound in Great Britain by
Collins, Glasgow

HEADLINE BOOK PUBLISHING PLC
Headline House
79 Great Titchfield Street
London W1P 7FN

With loving thanks to
Mum, Dad, Desmond and Debra

Contents

Introduction

Having just spent the last three years as a student I can say with confidence that food will play a major part in your life during your time at college. For many people it is their first experience of having to fend for themselves in the kitchen. Most people take up this challenge with great enthusiasm to discover that the art of cooking is not shrouded in the mystery that they had supposed. Also, I firmly believe that the more you cook the better you get at it. I remember especially the glee with which a friend of mine produced his first (inedible) casserole. His cooking rapidly improved – hunger is a great spur and as a student you will always be hungry – so that by the end of finals he could prepare an (edible) elaborate three-course meal for fifteen people. This blow-out was, incidentally, cooked under cramped cooking conditions in the tiny kitchen of a hall of residence where other students were also trying to cook for themselves.

Eating is at the centre of many social activities whether it be cooking meals with or for friends, or demolishing hastily assembled snacks at any time of the day or night. Some of my happiest college memories are of long evenings spent eating and drinking with friends.

The recipes in this book which sustained me through college also take heed of that important element in student life – money. None of the recipes will break the bank, and where some dishes are more expensive to produce I have indicated this. I have also included some recipes for when the money really does run out. I have also taken into account what cooking facilities may be available to you. This can be a major consideration when ten students are sharing – or fighting over – one cooker. With this in mind, some of the dishes are quick to cook and others are cook-in-one-dish recipes.

When I was at university I first of all lived in a self-catering hall of residence. Next I shared a flat with a friend, Lucy, who became infamous for her penchant for collecting milk bottles. As term wore on, entering and exiting from our flat became a hazardous exercise as one had to manoeuvre through the increasing pile of milk bottles outside our flat. She was always promising faithfully to remove them. Later I lived with a mixed group in a house. Each experience was completely different but the common thread was trying to fit in with each other.

Many students who start off living in a hall of residence quickly learn *the* most important rule, which is that anything that is not fastened down, or that does not have a 'keep off' notice on it, will get stolen, or if one is being polite, borrowed for the duration! For instance, you may come to eat your cornflakes in the morning and find yourself screaming about the – er – person who has stolen your milk. However, a few nights later this epithet may apply to yourself, when you arrive back late, with thirsty friends, to find that you have no milk but there is some in the fridge. . .

This explains why it was a not uncommon sight, especially during the colder months of the year, to see plastic carrier bags hanging from the handles of windows outside the hall of residence. The bags being instant refrigerators for various goodies. One tutor observed that where there was a student there were always plastic carrier bags. This might supply him with some sort of reason.

Some of you will be lucky and live near excellent supermarkets and greengrocers with reasonably priced goods. Others will find themselves stuck out on campuses with a shop whose prices are higher. Whatever your shopping facilities, you will need to buy as cheaply as possible the four staples of the student diet: bread, pasta, rice and potatoes. With these foods to build on you will certainly not starve – and most of the recipes in this book are based on these foods.

Since for some students fresh foods are difficult to buy – and store – many of the recipes use canned ingredients.

Canned foods do have advantages. Most of the work has already been done, there is no waste, and the varieties available are not subject to seasonal price fluctuations. You may be concerned about canned foods lacking in vitamins and 'goodness', and so on, but I can assure you that the modern canning processes keep all these elements firmly *in* the can. I know, since I had to look into the canning processes for one of my dissertations.

When you move from a hall of residence to that first 'place of your own' you will be able to become more adventurous in your cooking – introducing more fresh foods and building up a larger store cupboard. A well-stocked store cupboard enables you to have at hand a constant supply of basic ingredients of the recipes. Suggested items to start off your store cupboard are found on page 13. In hall, space is usually at a premium but when you are sharing a flat or a house you will have more storage space. When I moved into my first shared flat I immediately began to build up a collection of spices. Curries are so much better when you make up your own curry powder.

On this note you will notice that there is a preponderance of curry powder and garlic in the recipes. Students probably consume more garlic and curry powder than the rest of the country put together. I remember one boyfriend I had who I thought had bad breath. Before too long, I put two and two together and realized that I only noticed the bad breath after we had eaten. Yes, garlic was the culprit and once removed from our meals the problem went away. So beware of garlic if you think it is having an adverse effect on your love life.

It is as a student that many men discover that cooking is not a female preserve. In fact, I think some men turn out to be better cooks than women. At college I found many of them to be excellent cooks – amongst them my special foodmate, Nigel. So all of you males out there – get cooking, it is certainly an asset in snaring yourself a female.

The good thing about student cookery is that people are generally so grateful to be fed that they will usually not complain about anything that is put before them. Having friends to supper is a good time to experiment and try out new dishes. This is how many of the recipes in this book have come about. Do not believe the old adage about not trying out a dish for the first time when you are entertaining.

Do *enjoy* your cooking. There is hardly anything to beat the pleasure of sitting down with friends and loved ones to eat, drink and chat. Often as a student you will just want to feed yourself as quickly as possible, perhaps because of a pressing engagement with an essay. Balance these times with social eating and you will discover one of the greatest pleasures of life.

Things you will need

When compiling your list of items to take to college try to include as many as possible of the following. An important item to have is a one-person casserole dish which is used in many of the recipes.

Many students arrive at their digs or hall of residence on a Sunday evening when the shops are shut. Think ahead; you will want something to eat on the day you arrive and also something for breakfast the following morning. If space is at a premium when travelling to college make sure you take at least the items marked essential on the lists given below.

If you can persuade your parents to start off your store cupboard, you will have no trouble in easily knocking up wholesome dishes just by weekly buying of items such as canned tomatoes, sweetcorn, condensed soups, cheese, peppers, mushrooms, onions, yoghurt and tuna. But remember to replace your store items as they run out.

Items to take to college
one-person casserole dish
1 small and 1 large saucepan
   with lids
small frying, or omelette, pan
colander or large sieve
dinner and tea plate
1 breakfast bowl
1 cup or mug
cutlery

1 chopping knife
wooden spoon
cheese grater
egg cup
plastic bowl or box with lid
liquid measure
measuring spoons
tea-towel
can opener
skewers (for kebabs)

Basic store cupboard

COFFEE
TEA
SUGAR ⎱ ESSENTIAL
MARGARINE/BUTTER ⎰
EGGS

oil
wholemeal flour
brown rice
pasta
potatoes
salt and pepper
chilli powder

mustard
mixed herbs
Italian seasoning
garlic
curry powder
tomato purée
soy sauce

Handy hints

● The measures in all the recipes are approximate; nothing will go dreadfully wrong if you use slightly more or less of an ingredient than stated in the recipe. If you do not have a tablespoon you can use a teaspoon for your measuring: 3 teaspoons = 1 tablespoon.

● Quantities of seasonings are only given as a guide. You will soon learn to adjust them to your taste. *Warning*: if you are cooking a hot dish for the first time for friends, for example, curry or chilli con carne, *check first* whether they like it hot or mild. It is too late after you have added the chilli powder.

● Some recipes use canned pulses such as kidney beans, butter beans, chick peas, etc. It is much cheaper if you buy them dry, allow them to soak and boil them yourself. The catch is that you have to remember to soak them overnight and they do take a while to cook.
　　For those of you who want to save those extra pennies here is the method. The weight of the dried beans is half that of cooked beans so only half the amount stated in the recipe is needed. Soak the beans overnight. Drain and boil in fresh water for 10 minutes. Simmer for 1-1½ hours or until the beans are soft. (If you have forgotten to soak the beans boil them for 10 minutes, turn off the heat, cover and leave to soak for 1 hour.) *Do not* add any seasoning at this point as this lengthens the cooking time. Cook the beans as directed in the recipe.
　　Some beans do not require such a long cooking time and these are pointed out in individual recipes. Lentils need no preparation: just use as directed in the recipes.

● When heating up yoghurt, do so *very* gently or it will separate.

- Try to keep your fat, sugar and salt intake to a minimum. Through practice you can change your tastes. When I came to university I took both milk and sugar in tea and coffee, now I take neither in coffee and just a little milk in tea. If you have not already done so change to brown bread, spaghetti and rice. It is better for you and has so much more taste.

- Try not to buy too many perishable items when shopping, for example, meat. If an unexpected, or forgotten, invitation turns up you will only have wasted your money.

- If you do not use all the contents of a can at once, do not keep it in the can. Transfer it to a plastic or china bowl. If left in the can the contents can develop a metallic taste.

- Make sure you have some foil or clingwrap for wrapping up any leftover or unused vegetables, for example, peppers or onions. Store them, if possible, in a refrigerator.

- Items often go missing from communal refrigerators. Prime targets are milk, meat, butter and cheese. Some times casual thieves are deterred if you keep your foodstuffs in a plastic box with your name on it. This, however, will not deter the professional thief – you just have to be lucky to catch them. Never let them go if you are lucky enough to catch one – they will only consider you a sucker and continue stealing.

- Be enterprising when cooking. If you do not have the exact pan or dish that the recipe states, substitute with a similar dish. However, do be careful about checking whether dishes are flame-proof. If friends borrow your favourite, or one and only, casserole dish warn them that it is not flame-proof. I lost three casserole dishes at college through friends either trying to use them on direct heat or by putting hot dishes into cold water. It is better to let the dishes cool gradually.

- Be prepared to improvise: for example, a clean dry milk bottle makes a very good rolling-pin.

- If you are lucky enough to be given or are able to buy a toasting machine, this can come in very handy for making a breakfast or lunch snack. Most machines come with a recipe book. Our favourites were cheese and pickle or baked-bean sandwiches. Sweet toasted sandwiches can also be made with banana or apple. Toasted sandwiches are quick and easy to make and very filling. My friend Sue and I virtually lived off them one summer until my mother noticed her toasting machine had disappeared from home.

- Where a recipe states serve with rice or pasta, allow 2-3 oz (50-75 g) dry weight per person. Allow approximately 6-8 oz (150-200 g) bought weight or 2 oz (50 g) frozen vegetables per person.

The symbols found opposite certain recipes indicate:

⬡ this recipe uses only one dish during preparation

🕐 this recipe can be made in half-an-hour or less

1 The Quick Snack

Student life is different. You will rapidly discover that meals may not consist of breakfast, lunch and dinner taken at standard times. Some people I knew at college had their breakfast in the evening before they went to bed, claiming that it saved them time in the morning. Although I would not personally recommend this, it does show how your eating patterns can alter as a student.

There are many times when speed is of the essence in preparing a meal. The breakfast grabbed before lectures. The quick lunch squeezed in between tutorials. The hasty dinner gulped down before going out for the evening. The one thing you will quickly learn is that foods are very interchangeable. Because something is usually eaten at breakfast does not mean that it cannot be eaten at other times of the day. Muesli is a good example of this. Although usually taken as a breakfast cereal, it is also a useful snack meal at other times of the day, especially when time is taken to chop up some fresh fruit and add it to the normal bowlful.

With such things in mind, the following recipes can all be used at any time of the day or night. They are all so quick and easy to prepare that no student has the excuse, as many will often claim, that cornflakes are the only thing they have time to eat.

All the recipes in this chapter are for one person.

Muesli
Serves 1

> 3 tablespoons (45 ml) rolled oats
> 1 tablespoon (15 ml) bran flakes
> 1 tablespoon (15 ml) raisins
> 1 tablespoon (15 ml) mixed nuts
> 5 fl oz (150 ml) milk

Mix all the ingredients together and serve with the milk.

Muesli can be varied by adding any or all of the following: yoghurt; cottage cheese; honey; bananas; apples or dates.

Boiled eggs and soldiers
Serves 1

> 2 eggs
> 2 slices wholemeal bread
> yeast extract

Boil some water in a small saucepan. Add the eggs carefully and boil for 4 minutes. Toast the bread and spread with the yeast extract. Cut the toast up lengthways and serve with the eggs.

Scrambled cheesy eggs on toast
Serves 1

> 2 eggs
> 1 tablespoon (15 ml) milk
> salt and pepper
> 2 slices wholemeal bread
> dab margarine
> 1 oz (25 g) cheese, grated

Break the eggs into a small bowl. Add the milk and seasoning and beat lightly. Make the toast. Melt the margarine in a small saucepan and add the egg mixture. Scramble with a fork and when the eggs start to cook, add the cheese. Serve on toast.

Ham or mushrooms can be added in place of cheese. Serve with grilled bacon or sausages, fried tomatoes or mushrooms and boiled potatoes for a more substantial snack.

Omelette
Serves 1

    2 eggs
    pinch mixed herbs
    salt and pepper
    dab margarine

Beat the eggs with the seasoning. Melt the margarine in a small frying-pan. Add the egg mixture and swirl over the bottom of the pan. Draw the mixture from the side of the pan, allowing the uncooked mixture to run underneath and set. To serve, fold in half and slide on to a plate. Alternatively, add any of the following fillings before folding: grated cheese and onion; sweetcorn; fried mushrooms; cooked peas and ham; sliced tomatoes or diced cooked chicken.

Serve as a main meal with a salad or any cooked vegetables and boiled potatoes.

Baked beans on toast
Serves 1

Baked beans on toast is probably the most popular student dish. None the less it has much to commend it, being both filling and nutritious. A tasty variation is to add a few sultanas and ½ teaspoon (2.5 ml) curry powder. On the subject of curry powder, beware of swapping recipes with friends who have hotter tastes than yourself. One of my friends nearly killed us with a curry she cooked. We found out later she got the recipe from an Indian student who liked his curries hot.

    7-oz (200-g) can baked, barbecue or curried beans
    2 slices wholemeal bread

Toast the bread and at the same time warm the beans. Vary by serving with grilled bacon or sliced tomatoes on top or by covering the beans with grated cheese and placing under the grill until the cheese melts.

Pitta pizzas
Serves 1

 1-2 pittas
 tomato purée
 cheese, grated
 tomatoes, sliced

Heat the pittas under the grill. Remove and spread the tomato purée on the pitta. Top with the cheese and tomatoes. Grill until the cheese bubbles. Alternative toppings are mushrooms, cold meats, peppers, fried onions and Italian seasoning.

Summer pitta salads
Serves 1

 pittas
 Salad
 red or white cabbage, shredded
 tomato, sliced
 onion, sliced
 carrot, grated
 sunflower seeds (optional)
 Dressing
 1 teaspoon (5 ml) oil
 1 tablespoon (15 ml) tomato relish
 2 tablespoons (30 ml) tomato juice
 ½ teaspoon (2.5 ml) chilli powder

Mix the salad ingredients together and use to stuff the pittas. Mix the dressing ingredients together and pour into each pitta. The salad ingredients can be varied according to taste. Add chopped cooked hamburgers, chicken or other meats to the pitta for a more substantial salad.

Soups

Although it is a little more time-consuming to make your own soups, these are not only delicious but more filling than packet or canned varieties. The curried bean soup is a good alternative to use when the thought of baked beans on toast again turns your stomach.

Curried bean soup
Serves 1

> 1 small onion, finely chopped
> 1 oz (25 g) butter
> ½ teaspoon (2.5 ml) curry powder
> 1 teaspoon (5 ml) tomato purée
> 7-oz (75-g) can baked beans
> 5 floz (125 ml) water

Fry the onion in the butter until brown. Add the remaining ingredients and bring to the boil. Simmer for 5 minutes.

Lentil soup
Serves 1

> 1 small carrot, grated
> 1 small onion, finely chopped
> 1 tablespoon (15 ml) oil
> 1 oz (25 g) red split lentils
> 10 floz (250 ml) tomato juice *or* 1 tablespoon (15 ml)
>   tomato purée mixed with 10 floz (250 ml) water
> seasoning

Sauté the carrot and onion lightly in the oil. Add the lentils and cook for a minute. Add the liquid, cover and simmer for 15-20 minutes. Season to taste.

Tomato and orange soup
Serves 1

1 small onion, finely chopped
½ oz (15 g) butter
8-oz (200-g) can tomatoes, chopped
5 floz (125 ml) orange juice
½ teaspoon (2.5 ml) basil, dried
1 teaspoon (5 ml) tomato purée
salt and pepper

Fry the onion in the butter until brown. Add the remaining ingredients and season to taste. Bring to the boil. Reduce the heat and simmer for 5 minutes stirring occasionally.

Corn chowder
Serves 2

Do not worry about the lumps that appear when you add the potato powder to this soup. Keep stirring – they do disappear.

½ pint (325 ml) milk
½ pint (325 ml) water
2½ oz (65 g) instant potato powder
3 oz (75 g) cheese, grated
½ teaspoon (2.5 ml) mustard powder
7-oz (175-g) can sweetcorn and peppers
salt and pepper

Combine the milk and water and bring to the boil. Reduce the heat and add the potato powder stirring all the time until all the lumps are incorporated. Squash any persistent lumps against the side of the pan. Add the remaining ingredients and heat until the cheese has melted. Season well before serving.

Double-decker roll

Serves 1

> 1 wholemeal roll
> margarine *or* butter
> one from each of the following:
> (1) cheese, ham, tuna, garlic sausage
> (2) onion, pickle, cucumber, tomato

Make two slits in the roll and butter the inside of these slits. Insert the chosen fillings into each slit.

Club sandwich

Serves 1

> 3 slices wholemeal bread
> margarine *or* butter
> slice of chicken *or* ham
> few slices tomato
> drained tuna *or* salmon mixed with 1 teaspoon (5 ml) mayonnaise
> few slices cucumber

Butter two slices of the bread. Put one buttered slice on a plate and cover with chicken or ham. Add the tomato. Place the unbuttered bread slice on top. Add the tuna or salmon and the cucumber. Top with the other slice of bread.

Open sandwich

Serves 1

You will need a knife and fork to eat this sandwich.

> 1 slice wholemeal bread, buttered
> lettuce, shredded
> 1-2 tablespoons (15-30 ml) cottage cheese
> tomato, quartered
> few slices cucumber

Place the lettuce on bread, top with cottage cheese and decorate with tomato and cucumber.

2 Cooking for One

Much of student cooking is for one person, and for this you cannot beat convenience foods. For the quantities required they do not work out much more expensive than fresh foods and you save yourself time and trouble. 'Varsity pie' is a good example of the ideal dish for one using convenience foods. It takes only a few minutes to prepare, uses only one dish, and does not have to be looked after while cooking.

However, you will often find that you are sometimes using only half a can of tomatoes, ratatouille, etc., in preparing dishes. Try to use these up the next day and make sure you transfer the contents of a half-finished can to another container. When clearing out the refrigerator at the end of term I often used to find leftover tomatoes which had grown a woolly coat of mould.

Students do not often bother with puddings. The only times we ever had them were at Sunday lunch and at dinner parties. However, I have included a few pudding recipes at the end of this chapter that are cheap, easy and quick to prepare.

All the recipes in this chapter can be doubled in quantity if you are chumming up with a friend for a meal, or are feeling just plain greedy. If you are cooking for a larger group of people use recipes from Chapter 3, 'Cooking with Friends' as you will find they work out cheaper.

Varsity pie
Serves 1

5-oz (125-g) can condensed mushroom, tomato *or*
  vegetable soup
4 oz (100 g) canned sweetcorn
4-oz (100-g) can tuna, drained
2 slices wholemeal bread, spread with margarine/butter
1 oz (25 g) cheese, grated

Pre-heat the oven to 190°C/375°F/Gas 5. Mix the soup, sweet-corn and tuna together and put into a greased one-person casserole dish. Butter the bread and cut into four triangles. Place, buttered side up, on top of the sweetcorn mixture. Sprinkle the grated cheese on top and bake for 25 minutes.

Pasta ratatouille
Serves 1

1 small onion, sliced
1 courgette, sliced
½ green pepper, sliced
1 clove garlic, chopped
1 tablespoon (15 ml) oil
8-oz (250-g) can tomatoes drained
Italian seasoning
3 oz (75 g) pasta shapes, cooked
1½ oz (40 g) cheese, grated

Fry the vegetables and garlic in the oil until they begin to soften. Add the tomatoes and seasoning. Cook over a low heat for 15 minutes. Mix the ratatouille and pasta together. Put in a flame-proof dish and cover with cheese. Place under the grill until the cheese bubbles. Serve with pitta or garlic bread (*see page 81*).

Mushroom kebabs
Serves 1

few mushrooms ⎫
1 banana ⎭ cut into bite-sized pieces

Marinade/sauce
2 tablespoons (30 ml) natural yoghurt
2 tablespoons (30 ml) orange juice
1 teaspoon (5 ml) oil
1 teaspoon (5 ml) curry powder

Mix the marinade ingredients. Add the mushrooms and banana and leave to soak for at least 1 hour. Thread the mushrooms and banana on to a skewer and grill for 10 minutes. Meanwhile, heat the marinade gently to make the sauce. (If it is too thin thicken with a little tomato purée.) Serve on a bed of rice with sauce poured over. Serve accompanied by mango chutney or cucumber raita (*see below*).

Cucumber raita
Serves 1

This can be a helpful recipe to have at hand when serving curries with which you have been a little too generous with the curry powder. People have been known to eat leftover raita for breakfast.

cucumber, chopped
2 tablespoons (30 ml) natural yoghurt
mint to season (optional)

Mix all the ingredients together and serve chilled.

Fish pie
Serves 1

1 portion cod in cheese sauce
2 oz (50 g) peas
8 oz (200 g) made-up instant mashed potato
2 oz (50 g) cheese, grated

Cook the cod and peas. Pour the cod in sauce into a small ovenproof dish. Break up the fish into flakes with a fork. Add the peas. Top with the mashed potato. Sprinkle on the cheese and grill until the top is browned.

Tuna crisp
Serves 1

packet potato crisps
4-oz (100-g) can tuna, drained
½ 8-oz (200-g) can sweetcorn, drained
5-oz (125-g) can condensed mushroom soup

Divide the crisps equally. Crush half into small pieces and mix with the other ingredients. Place the mixture into an ovenproof dish and top with the remaining crisps. Cook at 190°C/375°F/Gas 5 for 25 minutes. Serve with toast.

Weekend chicken
Serves 1

1 portion chicken, fresh or thawed
4 oz (100 g) canned sweetcorn
6½-oz (180-g) can tomato cook-in-sauce
or 8 oz (200 g) canned tomatoes and small onion, sliced
    and a pinch of mixed herbs

Put the chicken and sweetcorn in an ovenproof dish and cover with the sauce. Cover the dish with foil and cook for 1-1½ hours at 180°C/350°F/Gas 4. Stir occasionally. Serve with rice or noodles.

Flied lice
Serves 1

4 oz (100 g) rice
2-3 slices bacon, rindless
few mushrooms
oil for frying
few cooked peas *or* some diced green pepper
4 oz (100 g) canned sweetcorn
1 egg, beaten
soy sauce

Put the rice on to cook. This takes approximately 20 minutes. Dice the bacon and fry gently. Quarter the mushrooms. When the rice is cooked, drain any water still in pan. Put a little oil in a frying-pan and heat gently. Add the rice, mushrooms, sweetcorn and peas or pepper. Mix well. Do not allow to stick to the pan. Make a little space in the bottom of the pan, add a little egg and as this cooks stir into the rice. Repeat until all the egg is cooked. Season with soy sauce.

One-person lasagne
Serves 1

14-oz (390-g) can ratatouille
2 slices pre-cooked lasagne
4 tablespoons (60 ml) natural yoghurt mixed with
    2 tablespoons (30 ml) grated cheese
1 oz (25 g) cheese, grated

Put a layer of ratatouille in an ovenproof dish; then one slice lasagne, then another layer of ratatouille and a layer of the cheese mixture, then another of the ratatouille and finally the other slice of lasagne. Cover with the remaining cheese mixture and top with the grated cheese. Cook for 45 minutes at 200°C/400°F/Gas 6. Serve with a tomato salad and garlic bread.

Vegetable and bacon risotto
Serves 1

> 2 rashers bacon, rindless and chopped
> 1 carrot, chopped
> 1 onion, chopped
> 2 mushrooms, chopped
> oil for frying
> 3 oz (75 g) cooked rice
> 1 cup stock

Fry the bacon and vegetables together in a little oil. Add the rice and fry for 1 minute. Add the stock and bring to the boil. Cover and simmer for 20 minutes or until all the stock has been absorbed. This dish can be served with a fried egg on top.

Pork and tomato hotpot
Serves 1

> 1 pork chop
> 6½ oz (180 g) canned tomato cook-in-sauce *or*
> 8-oz (200-g) can tomatoes, small sliced onion
>   and a pinch of mixed herbs
> 1 medium-sized potato, peeled and very thinly sliced

Place the chop in a saucepan. Pour the sauce over and arrange the potato slices on top. Cover tightly with a lid and simmer *very* gently for 1 hour. Serve with peas or any other green vegetable.

Baked cheese and tomato sandwich
Serves 1

2 slices wholemeal bread
dab margarine
½ teaspoon (2.5 ml) mustard, made up
1 tomato, thinly sliced
1 small onion, finely chopped
2 oz (50 g) cheese, grated
1 egg, beaten
4 fl oz (100 ml) milk
black pepper

Spread the bread with the margarine and mustard. Place one slice of bread in the bottom of an ovenproof dish. Add the tomato, onion and half the cheese. Top with the other slice of bread. Beat together the egg, milk and seasoning. Pour over the bread. Sprinkle the remaining cheese on top. Cook at 180°C/350°F/Gas 4 for 35 minutes.

Bean pilaff
Serves 1

3 oz (75 g) rice
1 oz (25 g) sultanas
½ green or red pepper
1 cup stock
8-oz (200-g) can butter beans
Sauce
1 tablespoon (15 ml) tomato purée
2 tablespoons (30 ml) natural yoghurt
1 teaspoon (5 ml) curry powder

Cook the rice, sultanas and pepper in the stock in a covered dish at 190°C/375°F/Gas 5 for 1 hour. Heat the butter beans. Mix the sauce ingredients and heat gently. Add the butter beans and heat through. To serve, pour the sauce over the cooked rice.

Boston baked beans
Serves 1

    3 slices bacon, rindless and cut into bite-size pieces
    7-oz (200-g) can barbecued beans

Fry the bacon, add the beans and heat through. Serve with rice.

Carrot and banana curry
Serves 1

    2 carrots, cut into thin 1-inch (2.5-cm) lengths
    1 small onion, sliced
    5 tablespoons (75 ml) orange juice + 5 tablespoons
      (75 ml) water
    small banana, sliced
    1 teaspoon (5 ml) curry powder
    2 tablespoons (30 ml) natural yoghurt

Boil the carrots and onion in the orange juice and water until tender (approximately 10 minutes). Add the banana and cook for a further minute. Add the curry powder and yoghurt and heat gently. Serve on a bed of rice.

Barbecued pork chop
Serves 1

    1 pork chop *or* spare rib
    1 small onion, chopped
    1 oz (25 g) butter
    1 tablespoon (15 ml) tomato purée *or* tomato ketchup
    1 tablespoon (15 ml) vinegar
    1 tablespoon (15 ml) brown sugar *or* honey
    dash soy sauce

Fry the pork and onion in the butter for 20 minutes. Remove the chop from the pan, add the rest of ingredients and cook for a couple of minutes. Return the pork to the pan and heat through. Serve with boiled or jacket potatoes and peas or sweetcorn.

Cauliflower cheese supreme
Serves 1

        small cauliflower, cooked and divided into florets
        few mushrooms, sliced
        1 egg, beaten
        small carton natural yoghurt
        2 oz (50 g) cheese, grated
        soy sauce

Mix the mushrooms and cauliflower together in an ovenproof dish. Mix the egg, yoghurt and half the cheese and season with soy sauce. Pour the sauce over the vegetables and cover with the rest of the cheese. Bake at 200°C/400°F/Gas 6 for 15-20 minutes. Serve with toast.

Sweet and sour vegetables
Serves 1

        1 onion
        ½ green pepper   } cut into 2-inch (5-cm) matchsticks
        1 carrot
        oil for frying
        4 oz (100 g) canned pineapple chunks
        Sauce
        2 tablespoons (30 ml) vinegar
        3 tablespoons (45 ml) brown sugar *or* honey
        1 teaspoon (15 ml) ground ginger
        ½ teaspoon (2.5 ml) flour
        ground black pepper
        1 tablespoon (15 ml) tomato ketchup *or* tomato purée

Stir-fry the vegetables until tender (approximately 5 minutes). Drain the pineapple chunks, reserving any juice, and add to the vegetables. Prepare the sauce by adding 2 tablespoons (30 ml) of the pineapple juice to the sauce ingredients. Add sauce to the vegetables and simmer gently for 2 minutes. Serve with noodles.

Tuna provençale
Serves 1

    1 small onion, chopped
    1 clove garlic, chopped
    oil for frying
    8-oz (200-g) can tomatoes, drained
    1 tablespoon (15 ml) tomato purée
    4-oz (100-g) can tuna, drained
    Italian seasoning
    8-oz (200-g) can sweetcorn and pepper, drained
    1 oz (25 g) cheese, grated

Fry the onion and garlic until soft. Stir in the tomatoes, purée, tuna and herbs and cook for 2 minutes. Put half the sweetcorn in the casserole dish and cover with half the tuna mixture. Add the remaining sweetcorn and then the tuna. Sprinkle cheese on top and cook at 190°C/375°F/Gas 5 for 30 minutes. Serve with toast.

Chicken Carter
Serves 1

    1 onion, chopped
    oil for fying
    4 oz (100 g) canned sweetcorn, drained
    ½ green pepper, sliced
    1 chicken portion, fresh or thawed
    3 tablespoons (45 ml) peanut butter
    1 cup chicken stock
    oil for frying

Fry the onion in a little oil until soft and put in an ovenproof dish with the sweetcorn and pepper. Brown the chicken in the frying-pan and place on top of the vegetables. Blend the peanut butter with a little stock. Add the remaining stock and pour over the casserole. Bake at 200°C/400°F/Gas 6 for 1-1½ hours. Serve with tagliatelle or rice garnished with a few peanuts.

Chinese chicken
Serves 1

    1 small onion, finely chopped
    1 clove garlic, chopped
    oil for frying
    1 small chicken breast, boned and thinly sliced
    ½ teaspoon (2.5 ml) ground ginger
    soy sauce
    ½ teaspoon (2.5 ml) brown sugar
    ½ carton fresh beansprouts

Fry the onion and garlic in a little oil until soft. Add the chicken, soy sauce, ginger and sugar. Stir-fry for 3 minutes. Add the beansprouts and cook for a further 2 minutes. Serve with rice or noodles.

Pauper's stroganoff
Serves 1

    ½ green pepper, sliced
    few mushrooms, sliced
    1 small onion, chopped
    1 oz (25 g) margarine
    1 teaspoon (5 ml) wholemeal flour
    soy sauce
    2 tablespoons (30 ml) natural yoghurt

Fry the pepper, mushrooms and onion in the margarine until soft. Stir in the flour and cook for 1 minute. Add the soy sauce and yoghurt and heat gently. Serve with rice or tagliatelle, sprinkled with paprika.

Kilty
Serves 1

    8-oz (200-g) can mince, *or* braised beef *or* steak and kidney
    ½oz (15 g) margarine
    1 tablespoon (15 ml) flour
    1 oz (25 g) cheese, grated
    1 tablespoon (15 ml) oats

Pre-heat the oven to 200°C/400°F/Gas 6. Warm up the meat in a small saucepan. Rub the margarine into the flour until it resembles fine breadcrumbs. Mix in the cheese and oats. Put the meat into a small casserole dish and top with the crumble. Bake in the oven for 25 minutes. Serve with a green vegetable and boiled potatoes.

Baked Spanish omelette
Serves 1

    1 tomato, chopped
    1 potato, cooked and diced
    ½ green pepper, chopped
    1 oz (25 g) cheese, grated
    2 eggs, beaten
    salt and pepper
    ½oz (15 g) butter

Pre-heat the oven to 220°C/425°F/Gas 7. Mix the vegetables and cheese together. Add the eggs to vegetables and season. Grease an ovenproof dish with the butter and pour in the omelette mixture. Bake until omelette sets (approximately 10-15 minutes). Serve with salad and boiled potatoes.

Fish crumble
Serves 1

    1 fish portion, cod *or* haddock
    5-oz (125-g) can condensed vegetable soup
    handful jumbo oats
    1 oz (25 g) cheese, grated

Pre-heat the oven to 180°C/350°F/Gas 4. Put the fish and soup into a small casserole dish. Mix the oats and cheese together and sprinkle topping over the fish and soup mixture. Cook for 35 minutes.

Curry pie
Serves 1

> 4 oz (100 g) minced meat
> 1 small onion, chopped
> oil for frying
> 1 teaspoon (5 ml) curry powder
> 1 tablespoon (15 ml) tomato purée
> 1 large potato, boiled and sliced

Cook the mince and onion in the oil until the meat is browned. Mix in the curry powder and tomato purée and turn into a small casserole dish. Cover with the cooked potato slices and bake for 30 minutes at 200°C/400°F/Gas 6.

Spaghetti with soup sauce
Serves 1

> 3 oz (75 g) wholemeal spaghetti
> few mushrooms, sliced
> dab margarine
> 1 sachet cup-of-soup

Cook the spaghetti and keep warm. Fry the mushrooms lightly in margarine. Make up the soup using only half of the amount of boiling water stated on the sachet. Mix the soup and mushrooms together and serve poured over the spaghetti.

Mustard lamb
Serves 1

> 2 teaspoons (10 ml) mustard, made up
> pinch mixed herbs
> 2 small lamb chops *or* 1 large chump chop

Mix the mustard and herbs together and spread thinly over both sides of the chops. Grill for 20 minutes, turning once. Serve with a green vegetable or salad and a jacket potato.

Fish kebabs
Serves 1

1 cod fillet portion, thawed and quartered
½ banana, cut into three pieces
1 tablespoon (15 ml) natural yoghurt
1 teaspoon (5 ml) cumin *or* curry powder
squeeze lemon juice

Marinate the fish and banana in the yoghurt, curry powder and lemon for at least 1 hour. Thread the fish and banana on to a skewer. Grill for 15 minutes. Serve with rice and mango chutney.

Stir-fried liver and carrot
Serves 1

4 oz (100 g) lamb's liver
1 carrot
small onion, chopped
oil for frying
dash soy sauce

Cut the liver and carrot into matchsticks. Fry the carrot, liver and onion in a little oil for 5 minutes. Add the soy sauce and cook for a further minute or two. Serve with rice.

Fish cakes
Serves 1

½ × 2½ oz (65 g) packet instant mashed potato
4-oz (100-g) can tuna *or* salmon, drained
salt and pepper
1 oz (25 g) breadcrumbs
oil for frying

Make up the instant potato with 3 fl oz (75 ml) hot water. Mix the potato and fish together. Season. Shape into two rounds and flatten. Coat with breadcrumbs and fry on both sides until brown. Serve with baked beans or a fried egg.

Liver with lemon and herbs
Serves 1

4 oz (100 g) lamb's liver
pinch mixed herbs
squeeze lemon juice
1 tablespoon (15 ml) cornflour mixed with 1 teaspoon
  (5 ml) paprika
½ tablespoon (7.5 ml) sugar
oil for frying

Cut the liver into long thin slices and mix with the other ingredients. Fry in a little oil for 7-8 minutes or until the liver is cooked. Serve with rice.

Onion and sausage rissoles
Serves 1

4 oz (100 g) sausage-meat
½ onion, finely chopped
salt and pepper
oil for frying

Mix the sausage-meat and onion and season. Shape into two flat rounds and fry in a little oil for 5 minutes on each side. Serve with baked beans or a fried egg.

Pork Chinese-style
Serves 1

1 pork chop
½ green pepper, cut into matchsticks
1 small onion, finely chopped
dash soy sauce
½ carton fresh beansprouts
oil for frying

Cut the flesh from the bone of the chop and cut up into very thin slices. Fry the pork, pepper and onion for 2 minutes. Add the soy sauce and beansprouts and cook for a further 2 minutes. Serve with rice.

Crispy chicken bake
Serves 1

⅟₂ packet crisps
1 chicken portion, fresh *or* thawed
1 tablespoon (15 ml) flour mixed with ⅟₂ teaspoon (2.5 ml)
   chilli powder
1 tablespoon (15 ml) tomato purée

Pre-heat the oven to 200°C/400°F/Gas 6. Crush the crisps into small pieces. Coat the chicken in the seasoned flour. Spread the tomato purée over the chicken before coating with the crisps. Bake in a casserole for 40 minutes. Serve with rice and cucumber raita (*see page 29*) or boiled potatoes and sweetcorn or peas.

Banana bake
Serves 1

1 banana, sliced
1 chocolate flake, crumbled
1 tablespoon (15 ml) mixed chopped nuts

Pre-heat the oven to 200°C/400°F/Gas 6. Layer the banana, chocolate flake and nuts into a small casserole dish. Bake for 15 minutes. Serve with cream or yoghurt.

Chocolate angel
Serves 1

⅟₂ packet chocolate flavoured whipped milk dessert
5 fl oz (150 ml) milk
1 chocolate flake, crumbled
2 tablespoons (30 ml) whipping or double cream

Make up the dessert with the milk. Mix in the crumbled flake. Whip the cream until it thickens slightly but do not overwhip. Place alternate layers of milk dessert and cream in a glass, finishing with a chocolate layer. Stir the top layer carefully so that traces of the cream layer below show through. Serve chilled.

Ginger cream
Serves 1

>   2-3 ginger biscuits
>   ½ packet peach-flavoured whipped milk dessert
>   5 fl oz (150 ml) milk

Crumble the ginger biscuits. Make up the whipped milk dessert. Place alternate layers of ginger crumbs and peach dessert in a dish. Chill for 5 minutes.

Fruit bake
Serves 1

>   6 oz (150 g) canned or stewed fruit
>   bran flakes, crushed
>   1 tablespoon (15 ml) brown sugar *or* chocolate flake

Place the fruit in an ovenproof dish. Mix the bran flakes with the brown sugar or a crumbled chocolate flake. Cook at 200°C/400°F/Gas 6 for 20 minutes.

3 Cooking with Friends

Many students live in student houses where everybody takes a turn at the cooking. Often there is a weekly kitty to pay for communal food items, such as milk, bread, tea, coffee and spices. Other cooking costs can then be easily split between you as they arise. However, if you are lucky enough to be sharing a house with a group of people who have similar tastes and appetites, a communal kitty can be organized which covers all food costs.

Living in a shared house means you no longer have to fight over the cooking facilities. You also have more storage space which means you can buy food in larger quantities which is more economical. With this in mind, the recipes in this chapter do not rely so heavily on canned ingredients. More use is made of fresh vegetables, and roughly one-third of the recipes in this chapter are vegetarian. Cheaper cuts of meat are also introduced. These are often difficult to obtain in small enough quantities for one, or require a long cooking time, which is inconvenient for people with limited cooking facilities. For example, sausages are included here, which may surprise some people who would have assumed that sausages are ideal for people cooking only for themselves. However, unless you can go to a butcher's most sausages can only be purchased by the pound. This means that if you purchased them in this quantity for one person only, you would have to eat sausages for three to four days in a row.

I have included some student versions of well-known dishes such as beef bourguignon, coq au vin and beef in beer. These recipes use cheap cuts of meat which need a long cooking time to produce good results. This is really only possible when you have proper cooking facilities – not one cooker which has to be shared between ten people.

When cooking in a shared house it is important to find out each other's likes and dislikes. This can prevent the unpleasant experience of everybody sitting down to eat only to find that one person cannot touch the food because it contains something he or she positively loathes.

This happened to me once. I had forgotten one of the boys I was sharing a house with could not drink cider as it made him violently ill – a result, we all thought, of over-indulgence at some former time. We had invited some friends round for a fondue and you should have seen his face when he tasted it. You see, to make it cheaper I had substituted cider for the wine. So he had to sit by with a sandwich while we all tucked into the beautiful fondue that he had been so looking forward to. The moral of this story is that it is perhaps wiser to check with people before making a dish. Just because you love something does not mean that everybody else will.

All the recipes in this chapter are for four people. They can be easily adjusted to suit three or even five people by using slightly more or less of the quantities given – or as dictated by appetites.

Dutch hot pot and bacon
Serves 4

Be warned that at some point in your culinary career you will experience 'the beans that won't cook'. Don't worry. It is something that happens to us all. I once cooked some beans for nearly three hours and they were still crunchy. If this does ever happen to you, I suggest you pretend you like crunchy beans and that they were supposed to turn out like that anyway.

>8 oz (200 g) red kidney beans, soaked overnight
>1 stock cube
>1 lb (400 g) potatoes, cubed
>2 carrots, cubed
>2 onions, sliced
>2 apples, cored and sliced
>1 green pepper, sliced
>4 oz (100 g) Gouda cheese, thinly sliced
>8-oz (200-g) packet bacon

Drain the beans and boil in fresh water for at least 10 minutes. Lower the heat and simmer for 30 minutes. Drain. Make up the stock with a stock cube and 1 pint (500 ml) water. Place the beans, apple and vegetables in a saucepan. Add the stock and cover the pan with a lid. Simmer for approximately 35 minutes until the vegetables are cooked and most of the liquid has been absorbed. Layer the Gouda over the top of the hot-pot and grill the bacon. When the bacon is done and the cheese has started to melt, serve the hot pot with the bacon and some crusty bread.

Sausages and onions
Serves 4

>2 large onions, sliced
>1 lb (450 g) pork sausages
>1 oz (25 g) butter
>soy sauce

Fry the onions and sausages gently in the butter for 25 minutes. Season with soy sauce and serve with barbecued beans and mashed or jacket potatoes.

Baked-bean lasagne
Serves 4

> 8 oz (200 g) cheese, grated
> 1 large onion, chopped
> 2 cloves garlic, crushed
> oil for frying
> 30 oz (800 g) baked beans, mixed with 2 tablespoons (30 ml) tomato purée
> 8 oz (200 g) or 12 pieces pre-cooked lasagne
> 1 packet cheese sauce, made up

Pre-heat the oven to 190°C/375°F/Gas 5. Reserve 2 oz (50 g) of the cheese for topping. Cook the onion and garlic in a little oil until soft and mix with the beans. Put a layer of beans in a large greased casserole dish, followed by a layer of cheese and then a layer of lasagne. Repeat the layering until all the ingredients are used up, finishing with a layer of lasagne. Top with the cheese sauce and sprinkle the reserved cheese on top. Bake for 35 minutes. Serve with tomato salad.

Fish casserole
Serves 4

> oil for frying
> 1 medium onion, chopped
> 1 green pepper, sliced
> 1 clove garlic, crushed
> 14-oz (400-g) can tomatoes
> 4 white fish fillet portions, cubed
> 12 oz (300 g) sweetcorn
> 2 slices wholemeal bread, crumbled
> handful bran *or* cornflakes
> 2 oz (50 g) cheese, grated

Fry the onion, pepper and garlic in a little oil until soft. Add the tomatoes and fish and cook for 5 minutes. Turn into a casserole dish with the corn. Cook for 20 minutes at 190°C/375°F/Gas 5. Mix the bread, cornflakes or bran and cheese together and sprinkle over the casserole. Cook for a further 10 minutes. Serve with jacket potatoes.

Fish creole
Serves 4

1 green pepper, sliced
1 red pepper, sliced
1 onion, sliced
oil for frying
16-oz (400-g) can tomatoes
1 teaspoon (5 ml) chilli powder
pinch mixed herbs
4 cod portions, thawed and flaked

Fry the peppers and onion in a little oil until soft. Add the tomatoes, seasoning and fish and simmer gently for 20 minutes. Serve with rice.

Coq au vin
Serves 4

1 onion, chopped
1 clove garlic, crushed
6 oz (150 g) streaky bacon, rindless
oil for frying
4 chicken portions, skinned
4 oz (100 g) mushrooms, sliced or quartered
1 cup red wine
8-oz (200-g) can tomatoes
pinch mixed herbs

Pre-heat the oven to 180°C/350°F/Gas 4. Fry the onion, garlic and bacon in a little oil until soft. Add the chicken and cook until browned. Transfer the fried ingredients to a casserole dish and add the rest of the ingredients. Cook in the oven for 1-1½ hours or until the chicken is cooked. Serve with boiled potatoes or noodles.

Liver with orange and paprika
Serves 4

1 large onion, chopped
1 clove garlic, crushed
oil for frying
1 lb (400 g) lamb's liver, sliced
flour for coating mixed with 1 tablespoon (15 ml) paprika
12 fl oz (350 ml) liquid made up of half water and half
   orange juice
pinch mixed herbs
2 teaspoons (10 ml) dark brown sugar

Fry the onion and garlic in a little oil until soft. Coat the liver with seasoned flour and brown in the pan. Stir in the liquid and herbs. Add the sugar and bring to the boil. Reduce the heat and simmer gently for 10-15 minutes. Serve with mashed potato or rice.

Cheese fondue
Serves 4

¾ pint (375 ml) white wine
1 lb (450 g) Cheddar cheese, grated
8 oz (225 g) gruyère *or* emmental cheese, grated
3 tablespoons (45 ml) or a miniature of vodka mixed with 4
teaspoons (20 ml) cornflour
crusty bread to serve

Heat the wine in a large saucepan or fondue pot. Add the cheeses and mix well. Cook for 5 minutes, stirring constantly. Add the vodka mixture and continue cooking, stirring all the time until the fondue thickens. If you have a fondue set serve at the table with squares of crusty bread for dipping. Otherwise serve the mixture in individual bowls, letting the rest of the fondue simmer very gently. Serve with big chunks of crusty bread.

Sussex potatoes
Serves 4

    4 medium/large baking potatoes (depending on appetites)
    4 bacon chops
    6 oz (150 g) cream cheese
    12-oz (300-g) can sweetcorn, drained
    salt and pepper
    butter *or* margarine

Pre-heat the oven to 220°C/425°F/Gas 7. Scrub the potatoes, prick the skin all over with a fork and bake for 1-1½ hours or until soft. Keep the potatoes warm when cooked. Grill the bacon chops and keep warm in the oven. Mix the cream cheese and the sweetcorn together. Season. Cut the potatoes in half and fork some butter or margarine into each half. Divide the cream cheese and corn mixture between the potatoes. Serve potatoes with the bacon chops.

Stuffed peppers
Serves 4

    4 large green peppers
    1 onion, chopped
    6 oz (150 g) mince
    oil for frying
    1 tablespoon (15 ml) tomato purée
    4 oz (100 g) cooked rice
    Italian seasoning

Blanch the peppers in boiling water for 1 minute. Allow to cool, then slice off the top and remove the insides. Fry the onion and mince until brown. Add the other ingredients and mix well. Stuff the peppers with the mixture. Cook for 40 minutes at 180°C/ 355°F/Gas 4. Serve with a green salad.

Ratatouille
Serves 4

3 cloves garlic, crushed
2 large onions, sliced
1 large aubergine, cubed
oil for frying
1 green pepper, sliced
3 courgettes, sliced
6 tomatoes, quartered
pinch mixed herbs
ground black pepper

Gently fry the garlic, onions and aubergine for 5 minutes. Add the other ingredients, cover and cook over a gentle heat for 40 minutes. For a thicker sauce, use canned tomatoes and tomato purée instead of fresh tomatoes. Serve with brown rice or wholemeal bread and parmesan cheese.

Beef in beer
Serves 4

If you don't have any brown ale, be careful what you use as a substitute. It tastes absolutely awful if you use lager.

1½ lb (600 g) stewing steak, cut into chunks
1 large onion, chopped
oil for frying
ground black pepper
2 large carrots, sliced
4 oz (100 g) mushrooms, sliced
1 cup brown ale
1 teaspoon (5 ml) vinegar
pinch mixed herbs

Pre-heat the oven to 160°C/325°F/Gas 3. Fry the beef and onion until the meat is browned. Season. Add the carrots and sliced mushrooms and cook for a few minutes. Turn into a casserole dish and add the rest of the ingredients. Stir. Cook in the oven for 2 hours. Check the casserole during cooking and add water or more ale if it is becoming too dry. Serve with mashed potatoes.

Barbecued ribs
Serves 4

2-2½ lb (1 kg) pork ribs
1 tablespoon (15 ml) honey *or* brown sugar
13-oz (376-g) can barbecue sauce
1 teaspoon (5 ml) chilli powder
1 tablespoon (15 ml) paprika

Pre-heat the oven to 180°C/350°F/Gas 4. Place the pork ribs in a roasting tin and cover with the honey or sugar. Cook for 30 minutes. Drain any excess fat from tin. Mix the chilli powder and paprika into the sauce and pour over the ribs. Cook for another 30 minutes. Serve with jacket potatoes and sour cream.

Fish fingers and onion sauce
Serves 4

12 fish fingers
Sauce
2 onions, sliced
oil for frying
1 oz (25 g) margarine
1 tablespoon (15 ml) wholemeal flour
pinch mustard powder
1 cup milk

Grill the fish fingers. Fry the onion in a little oil until soft. Make the sauce by melting the margarine and blending with the flour. Cook for 1 minute. Add the mustard and then the milk and bring to the boil, stirring constantly. Simmer until the sauce thickens, stirring all the time. Add the onions to the sauce and serve poured over fish fingers with peas and mashed potatoes.

Bean stew
Serves 4

15-oz (440-g) can kidney beans
15-oz (440-g) can borlotti beans in chilli sauce
15-oz (440-g) can butter beans
14-oz (400-g) can ratatouille
16-oz (400-g) can tomatoes + 2 tablespoons (30 ml)
    tomato purée

Drain the kidney and butter beans. Mix all the ingredients together and heat gently in a saucepan. Add seasonings to taste, for example, mixed herbs, Italian seasoning or chilli powder. Serve with brown rice.

Lentil and tomato bake
Serves 4

12 oz (300 g) red split lentils
1 large onion, chopped
oil for frying
2 tablespoons (30 ml) tomato purée
3 tomatoes, sliced
1½ lb (600 g) potatoes, cooked and sliced
5 fl oz (150 ml) natural yoghurt
3 oz (75 g) cheese, grated

Pre-heat the oven to 200°C/400°F/Gas 6. Fry the lentils and onion for 5 minutes. Cover with water and cook for 15-20 minutes until all the liquid is absorbed. Add the purée and mix well. Put half the mixture into a casserole dish. Cover with the tomatoes. Then add the remaining lentil mixture. Top with the potatoes. Pour the yoghurt over the potatoes and sprinkle the cheese on top. Cook for 30-40 minutes or until the top is brown. Serve with canned barbecue beans.

Devilled kidneys
Serves 4

> oil for frying
> 1 onion, chopped
> 8 lambs' kidneys, chopped
> 8-oz (200-g) can tomatoes
> 1 teaspoon (5 ml) Italian seasoning
> 1 teaspoon (5 ml) chilli powder

Fry the onion in the oil until soft. Add the kidneys and brown. Stir in the other ingredients. Bring to the boil, and allow to simmer gently for 10 minutes. Serve with rice.

Aubergines and tomatoes
Serves 4

> 2 aubergines, sliced
> oil for cooking
> 1 onion, sliced
> 1 clove garlic, crushed
> 14-oz (400-g) can tomatoes
> 1 tablespoon (15 ml) tomato purée
> 1 teaspoon (5 ml) Italian seasoning
> 5 fl oz (150 ml) natural yoghurt
> 3 oz (75 g) cheese, grated

Pre-heat the oven to 180°C/350°F/Gas 4. Fry the aubergines in 2 tablespoons (30 ml) oil until golden brown and remove from the pan. Fry the onion and garlic until soft. Add the tomatoes, purée and seasoning and simmer for 5 minutes. Put alternate layers of tomato mixture and aubergines into a casserole dish, finishing with a layer of aubergine. Cover with yoghurt and sprinkle the cheese on top. Cook in oven for 30-40 minutes. Serve with rice.

Hot and spicy chicken
Serves 4

1 lb (400 g) onions, finely chopped
2 cloves garlic, crushed
oil for frying
8-oz (200-g) can tomatoes
2 tablespoons (30 ml) tomato purée
1 tablespoon (15 ml) paprika
4 chicken portions, skinned

Fry the onion and garlic very gently in a large saucepan for 15 minutes. Add the tomatoes, purée and seasoning. Add the chicken and coat thoroughly in the sauce. Place the lid on the pan and simmer gently 45 minutes or until the chicken is cooked. Serve with jacket potatoes and sour cream.

Cheese and onion quiche
Serves 4

8-oz (200-g) packet shortcrust pastry, thawed
1 large onion, chopped
oil for frying
3 large eggs
4 fl oz (125 ml) single cream
ground black pepper
4 oz (100 g) cheese, grated

Pre-heat the oven to 190°C/375°F/Gas 5. Line a greased 8-inch flan dish with the pastry. Fry the onion until soft and put in the flan case. Beat the eggs and add the cream and seasoning. Pour over the onions and sprinkle the cheese on top. Cook for 30 minutes or until the mixture has set. Serve with boiled potatoes.

Beef bourgie
Serves 4

>1 large onion, sliced
>8 oz (200 g) streaky bacon, rindless and chopped
>1½ lb (600 g) stewing steak, cubed
>oil for frying
>4 oz (100 g) mushrooms, sliced
>ground black pepper
>pinch mixed herbs
>1 cup red wine

Pre-heat the oven to 160°C/325°F/Gas 3. Fry the onion, bacon and beef until brown. Put in a greased casserole dish and add the remaining ingredients. Cook for 2 hours. Check during cooking and add water, or a little more wine, if the casserole is becoming too dry. Serve with noodles.

Shepherd's pie
Serves 4

I hope you know the difference between mincemeat and minced meat. I once heard an awful story about someone who used mincemeat in shepherd's pie. It did not turn out very well.

>1 onion, chopped
>oil for frying
>1 lb (400 g) mince
>10-oz (250-g) can condensed oxtail soup
>3 oz (75 g) packet instant potato

Fry the onions until brown. Add the mince and fry until cooked through (approximately 20 minutes). Mix in the soup and heat thoroughly. Put the meat into a greased pie-dish. Make up the instand potato and use to top the pie. Place under the grill until the mash is golden brown. Serve with carrots.

Cottage pie

Use condensed vegetable in place of oxtail soup and add 2 oz (50 g) grated cheese to the instant potato.

Veggie pie

Substitute 4 oz (100 g) mushrooms and 1 lb (400 g) cubed aubergine in place of the mince and proceed as for shepherd's pie.

Hummus and chilli sauce
Serves 4

> Hummus
> 15-oz (440-g) can chick peas, drained
> 2 teaspoons (10 ml) cumin or curry powder
> 2 cloves garlic, crushed
> pinch salt
> 2 tablespoons (30 ml) oil
> 4 tablespoons (60 ml) lemon juice
> ground black pepper
> Sauce
> 1 onion, chopped
> 2 cloves garlic, crushed
> 2 tablespoons (30 ml) oil
> 1 teaspoon (5 ml) chilli powder
> 2 tablespoons (30 ml) tomato purée
> 14-oz (400-g) can tomatoes
> pinch mixed herbs

Mash the chick peas to a purée with the cumin or curry powder, garlic and salt. Pass the purée through a sieve. Blend in the oil and lemon and season well. Make the sauce by frying the onion and garlic in the oil until soft. Add all the other ingredients and bring to the boil. Allow to simmer for 10 minutes, stirring occasionally. Serve the sauce poured over the hummus accompanied by pittas or rice.

Spaghetti with mushrooms and walnuts
Serves 4

> 12 oz (300 g) wholemeal spaghetti
> 1 onion, chopped
> 2 cloves garlic, crushed
> oil for frying
> 16-oz (400-g) can tomatoes
> 8 oz (200 g) mushrooms, sliced
> 4 oz (100 g) walnuts, chopped

Cook the spaghetti in boiling salted water. Fry the onion and garlic in a little oil until soft and add the rest of ingredients. Continue to cook until the spaghetti is ready (approximately 10 minutes). Serve the sauce poured over the spaghetti with parmesan cheese.

Mushroom flan

Serves 4

> *Flan*
> 6 oz (150 g) wholemeal flour
> pinch salt
> 4 oz (100 g) margarine
> 2 tablespoons (30 ml) water
> *Filling*
> 8 oz (200 g) mushrooms, sliced
> 1 large onion, chopped
> oil for frying
> 2 eggs, beaten
> 4 oz (100 g) curd cheese
> 4 fl oz (125 ml) single cream

Make the flan pastry by rubbing the margarine into the flour and salt until it resembles breadcrumbs. Bind into a dough with a little water. Roll out carefully to line an 8-inch flan case. Chill. Fry the onion and mushrooms in the oil until soft. Beat the eggs, cheese and cream together and add in the mushrooms and onion. Pour the mixture into the flan case and bake at 180°C/375°F/Gas 5 for 35 minutes. Serve with potato salad and tomatoes

Spaghetti with tuna sauce

Serves 4

> 12 oz (300 g) wholemeal spaghetti
> 1 packet seafood soup
> 8-oz (200-g) can tuna, drained
> 12-oz (300-g) can sweetcorn, drained

Cook the spaghetti in boiling salted water. Make up the soup using only 15 fl oz (425 ml) water. Add the tuna and sweetcorn to the soup and mix well. Heat through and serve on the spaghetti with parmesan cheese.

4 The Occasional Sunday Roast

One meal which in my experience students often yearn for is a traditional roast dinner. Often a group of friends band together to satisfy this longing. However, such a meal needs planning. You must agree the number of people who wish to participate so you can work out how much food is needed. Then some brave souls must volunteer to actually get up on time on a Saturday morning to go and get the shopping. You would be surprised how much sleep people claim they need after a hectic week of lectures, drinking, tutorials and, yes, more drinking. It is best to break the participants up into groups of either two or three, depending on how many are catered for. If, for instance, there are six of you, two could do the shopping, with a pre-made list, two could do the cooking and two would be left to wash and dry up after the meal.

All organizational obstacles safely out of the way, you should be all set to enjoy one of the great pleasures of life. It is when you can actually smell the joint cooking that you know that the trouble taken has been worthwhile.

Traditionally, this was one meal for which we always got in a few bottles and made real pigs of ourselves by having a pudding as well. Sundays really feel like Sundays when you have to lie down after dinner with that contented full feeling. So that the vegetarians amongst us do not feel left out, I have included my favourite nut roast recipe in this chapter, which has always gone down well even with the hardiest of meat-eaters.

For these classic roasts I have given an additional vegetable dish and a traditional accompaniment to serve with the roast. (I have also suggested beverages, but these are obviously a matter of personal choice.) Serve roast potatoes, peas and gravy to accompany. The roast potatoes can be replaced with boiled new potatoes in the summer.

Gravy is very easy to make from packet mixes. Just follow the instructions on the packet. The same goes for peas, for which the cooking instructions will be on the container in which you buy them. The average portion of peas per person is 2 oz (50 g).

You will need at least one roasting dish for these dinners. If you do not have one, club together with your friends to buy one. It is also worth buying a large self-basting dish. These have lids with dimples on them in which the fat collects, and then drips back on to the cooking joint. The lid should be removed for the last 30 minutes of cooking time to allow the joint to brown properly.

Menu
Roast pork
Roast potatoes
Baked parsnips
Peas
Apple sauce
Gravy
Ginger pear trifle
Drink: cider

Roast pork
Serves 5-6

> 3 lb (1.25 kg) joint of pork (loin, leg or shoulder)
> oil or lard for basting
> garlic (optional)

Pre-heat the oven to 200°C/400°F/Gas 6. Rinse the joint and pat dry. Score the rind by taking a sharp knife and cut 2-inch (5-cm) gashes about 1 inch (2.5 cm) apart all over the rind. Brush with oil and season. Roast for an initial 35 minutes, then for 35 minutes per 1 lb (500 g) (approximately 2½ hours for a 3 lb (1.25 kg) joint). Baste very occasionally. If very crisp crackling is required, turn up the heat for the last 15-20 minutes of the cooking time. The crackling must be removed before carving.

Serve accompanied by apple sauce. This can be bought in cans or jars. Alternatively, make your own by stewing two sliced apples in a little water until pulpy, then flavouring with a squeeze of lemon juice, 1 teaspoon (5 ml) sugar and a pinch of allspice.

Roast potatoes

8 oz (200 g) potatoes per person
oil or lard for cooking

Wash and scrape the potatoes while bringing some salted water to the boil. Cut the potatoes into even-sized pieces and boil in the water for 5-10 minutes or until they lose a little of their hardness. Drain and sprinkle with salt and pepper. Cook around the roast for 1-1½ hours.

Baked parsnips
Serves 5-6

1 lb (400 g) parsnips
2 oz (50 g) lard *or* 3 tablespoons (45 ml) oil

Cut off both ends of the parsnips and peel. Slice in half lengthways and par-boil as for roast potatoes (see above) for 5-10 minutes. Bake with fat in a roasting dish at 200°C/400°F/Gas 6 for 1-1½ hours. Baste occasionally.

Ginger pear trifle
Serves 4-6

1 ginger cake
1 cup cider *or* pear juice
16-oz (400-g) can pears *or* 4 bananas, sliced
1-1½ pints (500-750 ml) made-up custard, cold
1 chocolate flake
nuts or glacé cherries to decorate

Slice up the cake and use to line the bottom of a large dish. Pour the cider or pear juice over the cake. Arrange the fruit on top. Pour the custard over the fruit. Chill until ready to serve. Crumble the flake over the top and decorate with nuts or cherries.

Menu
Roast lamb
Mint sauce
Stuffed mushrooms
Roast potatoes
Peas
Gravy
Apple and rhubarb crumble
Drink: red wine

Roast lamb
Serves 5-6

2-2½ lb (1 kg) joint of lamb (leg, loin or shoulder)
oil *or* lard for basting
salt and pepper
rosemary (optional)

Pre-heat the oven to 200°C/400°F/Gas 6. Rinse the joint and pat
dry. Brush the joint with oil and season. Roast for 35 minutes per
1 lb (500 g) (approximately 1-1½ hours for a 2 lb/1 kg joint). Baste
occasionally.

Serve accompanied by mint sauce. This can be bought
ready-made or made with chopped mint, sugar, water and
vinegar.

Stuffed mushrooms

1 packet stuffing mix
1 oz (25 g) butter
3 large, flat mushrooms per person

Make up the stuffing as directed on the packet using the butter.
Remove the stalks from the mushrooms, chop and mix with the
stuffing. Spread the stuffing on each mushroom, pressing down
lightly. Bake in a greased ovenproof dish with the roast for 15
minutes before serving.

Apple and rhubarb crumble
Serves 5-6

- 16-oz (400-g) can apple
- 16-oz (400-g) can rhubarb
- 2 oz (50 g) margarine
- 4 tablespoons (60 ml) wholemeal flour
- 2 tablespoons (30 ml) jumbo oats
- 2 tablespoons (30 ml) brown sugar

Place the fruit in a greased baking dish. Rub the fat into the flour until it resembles breadcrumbs. Add the other ingredients to the crumble and mix. Sprinkle the topping over the fruit. When the roast is cooked put the crumble in the oven at 200°C/400°F/Gas 6 to bake for approximately 20-25 minutes. Serve hot.

Menu
Roast beef
Yorkshire pudding
Cauliflower cheese
Roast potatoes
Peas
Gravy
Rice pudding
Drink: red wine

Roast beef
Serves 5-6

> 3 lb (1.25 kg) joint beef (back rib, topside or silverside)
> oil *or* lard for basting
> salt and pepper
> mustard (optional)

Pre-heat the oven to 220°C/425°F/Gas 7. Rinse the joint and pat dry. Brush the joint with oil and season. Roast for 1 hour for rare meat (15 minutes plus 15 minutes per l lb/500 g), or 1 hour 20 minutes for medium meat (20 minutes plus 20 minutes per 1 lb/500 g). For well-done meat cook for 1 hour 40 minutes (25 minutes plus 25 minutes per 1 lb/500 g). Baste occasionally.

Yorkshire pudding
Serves 5-6

> 4 oz (100 g) plain flour
> pinch salt
> 1 egg, beaten
> ½ pint (300 ml) milk
> dripping, lard *or* oil

Sift the flour and salt into a mixing bowl. Make a well in the centre of the flour and pour in the egg and half the milk. Draw the flour into the liquid and mix until a thick batter is formed. Gradually beat in the rest of the milk. Put a little fat into each of the holes in a twelve-hole bun tin. Put the tin into the oven for a few minutes to heat the oil. Fill the bun tin with the batter. Cook with the roast for 20 minutes, or until the puddings are golden.

Cauliflower cheese
Serves 4-6

> 1 large cauliflower
> *Cheese sauce*
> 1 oz (25 g) butter
> 2 tablespoons (30 ml) flour
> ½ pint (300 ml) milk
> 5 oz (125 g) cheese, grated
> salt and pepper

Wash the cauliflower and divide into florets. Cook in boiling salted water for 10 minutes. Drain. Prepare the sauce by melting the butter in a saucepan. Blend in the flour and cook for 1 minute, stirring continuously. Remove from the heat and add the milk slowly, stirring all the time. Return to the heat and bring slowly to the boil. Add 3 oz (75 g) of the cheese and season with salt and pepper. Put the cauliflower into a casserole dish and pour the cheese sauce over. Sprinkle the remaining cheese on top and bake with the roast for 15-20 minutes.

Rice pudding
Serves 4-6

> 4 oz (100 g) short-grain pudding rice
> 1½ pints (900 ml) milk
> 2 oz (50 g) sugar
> 1 tablespoon (15 ml) sultanas or raisins
> 1 eating apple, chopped
> ¼ teaspoon (1 ml) cinnamon
> few knobs of butter

Put the rice and the milk into a saucepan, bring to the boil and allow to simmer for 10 minutes. Put the sugar, sultanas and apple into a greased shallow ovenproof dish. Pour the rice and milk over. Sprinkle the cinnamon over the dish. Dot with knobs of butter. Carefully place in the oven with the roast 30 minutes before the joint is due to come out. When the joint is cooked and a skin has formed on the pudding, turn the heat down to 170°C/325°F/Gas 3 and continue cooking for a further 30 minutes. Serve with condensed milk.

Menu
Roast chicken
Sage and onion stuffing
Corn fritters
Roast potatoes
Peas
Gravy
Jam roly-poly
Drink: white wine

Roast chicken
Serves 5-6

4½ lb (2 kg) roasting chicken
oil *or* lard for basting
salt and pepper

Pre-heat the oven to 220°C/425°F/Gas 7. Remove the giblets from the chicken. Rinse the bird and pat dry. Brush with oil and season. A knob of butter can be placed inside the chicken to keep it moist during cooking. Roast for 1½-2 hours. To check whether it is cooked, prick the flesh so that the juices run out. If the juices are pink the chicken requires more cooking; if clear, it is done.

Sage and onion stuffing
Use a ready-made stuffing mix and make up as directed on the packet.

Corn fritters
Makes 10-12

>4 oz (100 g) wholemeal flour
>8 tablespoons (120 ml) water
>12 oz (300 g) sweetcorn
>oil for frying

Blend the flour and water together. Add the sweetcorn. Cook 2-3 fritters at a time by placing 2-3 tablespoons (30-45 ml) of the mixture in an oiled frying-pan. Cook, turning once, until the fritters are brown on each side (approximately 3 minutes).

Jam roly-poly
Serves 4-6

>6 oz (150 g) self-raising flour
>pinch salt
>3 oz (75 g) shredded beef suet
>3-4 tablespoons (45-60 ml) hot water
>12 oz (300 g) jam

Sift the flour and salt into a mixing bowl. Stir in the suet and gradually add the water until a soft dough is formed. Do not add more water than specified above. Knead the dough until smooth and roll out into an oblong about ½ inch (1 cm) thick. Spread half the jam along the dough, leaving a margin round the edge. Roll up like a swiss roll from one of the short sides. Pinch and seal the edges with a little water. Wrap loosely in well-greased foil. Seal well. Steam in a metal colander over a saucepan of boiling water for 2 hours. Keep topping up the water level during steaming. Before serving, heat the remaining jam in a small pan and serve poured over the roly-poly.

Menu
Roast gammon
Glazed pineapple
Spiced carrots
Roast potatoes
Peas
Gravy
Rich bread and butter pudding
Drink: cider

Roast gammon
Serves 5-6

> 3 lb (1.25 kg) gammon joint
> 1 bouquet garni
> salt and pepper
> 2 tablespoons (30 ml) honey

Soak the joint overnight in water. Drain the gammon and place in a large saucepan. Cook with the bouquet garni for 1½ hours. Remove from the pan and rinse under cold water. Cut off the rind and some of the fat covering the flesh. Score the remaining fat in a diamond pattern. Season and brush with the honey. Pre-heat the oven to 220°C/425°F/Gas 7 and roast for 20 minutes until the joint is glazed and crisp.

Glazed pineapple
Serves 5-6

> 11-oz (275-g) can pineapple slices
> 2 oz (50 g) butter
> 2-3 tablespoons (30-45 ml) brown sugar

Fry the pineapple slices in the butter and brown sugar until glazed. Warm in the oven with the roast.

Spiced carrots
Serves 5-6

> 1 lb (400 g) carrots
> 1 oz (25 g) butter
> 3 fl oz (75 ml) cider *or* orange juice
> 3 fl oz (75 ml) water
> 1 teaspoon (5 ml) rosemary
> 1 teaspoon (5 ml) mustard powder (optional)

Top and tail the carrots and slice thinly into 1-inch (2.5-cm) lengths. Melt the butter, add the carrots and cook gently for 5 minutes. Add the liquid. Add the rosemary, and mustard if using. Bring to the boil and cover the pan. Simmer gently for 10 minutes, adding more water if needed. Drain the carrots, reserving the liquid. Boil the liquid until reduced to a syrup. Serve the syrup poured over the carrots.

Rich bread-and-butter pudding
Serves 4-6

> 2 oz (50 g) glacé cherries
> 3 tablespoons (45 ml) whisky *or* 2 fl oz (60 ml) orange juice
> 4 oz (100 g) sultanas
> 10 slices bread, buttered
> 1 oz (25 g) brown sugar
> 4 eggs, beaten
> 1 ½ pints (900 ml) milk

Chop the cherries and soak in the whisky or orange juice with the sultanas for 15 minutes. Cut the bread into triangles and use to line a greased ovenproof dish. Sprinkle the fruit, sugar and whisky or juice on the bread. Place the remaining slices of bread on top. Beat the eggs and milk together and pour over the bread. When the joint is cooked bake in the oven at 220°C/425°F/Gas 7 for 45 minutes. Serve hot.

Menu
Stuffed nut roast
Cranberry sauce
Brussels sprouts with almonds
Roast potatoes
Peas
Banana cake
Drink: red wine

Stuffed nut roast
Serves 5-6

Nutmeat
4 oz (100 g) pine kernels
2 oz (50 g) cashews
2 oz (50 g) almonds
1 onion, chopped
1 oz (25 g) butter
4 tablespoons (60 ml) milk
2 eggs, beaten
4 oz (100 g) wholemeal breadcrumbs
salt and pepper
nutmeg
Stuffing
1 sachet country stuffing
4 oz (100 g) mushrooms, chopped
1 oz (25 g) butter
1 clove garlic, crushed
soy sauce
pinch mixed herbs

Pre-heat the oven to 200°C/400°F/Gas 6. Grease a 1-lb loaf-tin very well. Grind the pine kernels, cashews and almonds. Make the nutmeat by cooking the onion in the butter until soft. Mix in all the other ingredients. Make up the stuffing as directed on the packet. Cook the mushrooms in the butter for a few minutes with the crushed garlic. Add to the stuffing and season with soy sauce and herbs. Put half the nutmeat into the tin and press down well. Cover with the stuffing and top with the rest of the nutmeat. Cover with foil and cook for 1 hour. To brown the top, remove the foil and cook for a further 10 minutes. Cool in the tin for 5 minutes before turning out.

Cranberry sauce
Use ready-made sauce or, if fresh cranberries are available, cook in very little water, or orange juice, in a saucepan over a very gentle heat until soft and mushy.

Brussels sprouts with almonds
Serves 5-6

    1½ lb (600 g) brussels sprouts
    2 oz (50 g) almonds, flaked
    1 oz (25 g) butter

Prepare the sprouts by cutting off the stalks and removing the outer leaves. Cut a slit in the bottom of each sprout. Cook in salted boiling water for 10 minutes. Toast the almonds in the grill tray. Watch carefully, as they burn easily. Drain the sprouts and return to the pan. Add the butter and when the sprouts are coated with melted butter add the almonds.

Banana cake
Serves 6-12

    8 oz (200 g) margarine
    4 oz (100 g) dark brown sugar
    3 eggs, beaten
    1 lb (400 g) ripe bananas
    12 oz (300 g) wholemeal flour
    1 tablespoon (15 ml) baking powder
    2 oz (50 g) sultanas
    chocolate spread and banana slices to decorate

Pre-heat the oven to 200°C/400°F/Gas 6. Grease a 7-inch cake-tin. Cream the margarine and sugar together. Add the eggs and beat well. Sieve the flour and baking powder together and fold into the mixture. Mash half the bananas and add to the mixture. Chop the remaining bananas and add to the mixture with the sultanas. Mix well. The mixture should be a dropping consistency. If it seems too dry, add a little milk. Turn into the cake-tin and cook for 50-60 minutes, or until a skewer pushed in the top comes out clean. Cool in the tin for 15 minutes, then remove carefully. When cool, cover the top with chocolate spread and decorate with banana slices. A little lemon juice sprinkled over the banana slices will prevent them from going brown.

5 Classic Student Dishes

There are some dishes that never lose their appeal among students, for example, spaghetti bolognese, curry and moussaka. What these dishes have in common is that they are easy to prepare and cheap to cook in large amounts. You may come up against these classics in different guises. I remember once at a friend's house where we had gathered to eat and watch the results of a by-election, a mouthwatering vegetable goulash was served up with the unappetizing name of 'by-election slops' (it was delicious, notwithstanding its name).

For an informal gathering of friends, students rarely bother with a pudding. Sometimes cheese and biscuits are provided, or fruit in season. We used to leave the cheese on offer all evening so that people could nibble, though they had just been adequately fed, as and when their appetites dictated. It is my experience that most students eat like gannets.

There will be times when you will want to satisfy your sweet tooth or indulge your friends. I have included in this chapter my version of chocolate fudge cake, always a very popular choice. The same holds for cheesecake (people always assume that you have spent hours slaving over a hot stove to create this delicacy). This version is very quick to prepare, but will make you feel quite smug when you present it. Also included is a recipe for a birthday cake. I have yet to meet a student who does not celebrate birthdays.

Garlic bread
Serves 4-6

This recipe can establish your reputation as a student cook and enhance your social life. There can be no other smell more guaranteed to get people's tastebuds going.

> mixed herbs
> 2 cloves garlic, crushed
> 4 oz (100 g) softened butter
> 1 french loaf
> poppy seeds

Pre-heat the oven to 200°C/400°F/Gas 6. Mix a pinch of mixed herbs with the garlic and butter. Slice the loaf at about 1-inch (2.5-cm) intervals to within ½ inch (1 cm) of the base. Open up the cuts and spread with the garlic butter. Close the cuts and smear a little butter over the top. Sprinkle poppy seeds on top of the loaf. Wrap in foil and cook for 20-30 minutes. Serve hot.

Spaghetti bolognese
Serves 4-6

> 32 oz (800 g) canned tomatoes
> 2 onions, chopped
> 2 cloves garlic, crushed
> oil for frying
> 1½ lb (600 g) minced meat
> 6 oz (150 g) mushrooms, sliced
> 1 tablespoon (15 ml) wholemeal flour
> 3 tablespoons (45 ml) tomato purée
> 1 teaspoon (5 ml) Italian seasoning
> salt and pepper
> 1 lb (400 g) wholemeal spaghetti

Drain the tomatoes, reserving 1 cup of the juice. Fry the onion and garlic in a little oil until soft. Add the mince and cook until brown. Add the mushrooms, flour and purée. Cook for 1 minute. Add the tomatoes, juice and seasoning. Cover and cook gently for 15-20 minutes while the spaghetti is cooking. Serve with parmesan cheese and garlic bread.

Chilli con carne
Serves 4-6

32 oz (800 g) canned tomatoes
2 onions, chopped
2 cloves garlic, crushed
oil for frying
1½ lb (600 g) minced meat
1 tablespoon (15 ml) wholemeal flour
2-3 tablespoons (30-45 ml) tomato purée
1-3 teaspoons (5-15 ml) chilli powder, according to taste
1 green pepper, chopped
1½ lb (600 g) kidney beans, cooked

Drain the tomatoes, reserving 1 cup of the juice. Fry the onion and garlic in a little oil until soft. Add the mince and cook until the meat is browned. Add the flour, purée, chilli powder, according to taste, and some of the tomato juice. Mix well. Add the tomatoes and pepper. Add the beans and stir well. If using canned beans, drain before use. Cover and simmer for 30 minutes. At the end of the cooking time, add more purée if the dish is too liquid, or more tomato juice if too dry. Serve with rice, crackers or pittas.

Lasagne
Serves 5-6

> 12 pieces pre-cooked lasagne, enough for two layers
> *Meat sauce*
> 2 onions, chopped
> 2 cloves garlic, crushed
> oil for frying
> 1 lb (400 g) minced meat
> Italian seasoning
> salt and pepper
> 16-oz (400-g) can tomatoes
> 3 tablespoons (45 ml) tomato purée
> *Cheese sauce*
> 2 eggs, beaten
> 5 fl oz (125 ml) natural yoghurt
> 10 oz (250 g) curd cheese
> 4 oz (100 g) cottage cheese
> *Topping*
> 4 oz (100 g) cheese, grated

Pre-heat the oven to 190°C/375°F/Gas 5. Make the meat sauce by frying the onion and garlic in a little oil until soft. Add the mince and cook until the meat is browned. Add the seasonings, tomatoes and purée. Simmer gently for 10 minutes.

Make the cheese sauce by beating the eggs and yoghurt together. Gradually blend in the curd and cottage cheeses.

Put a layer of the meat sauce over the bottom of a shallow, greased casserole dish. Cover with half the lasagne, then another layer of meat sauce, followed by a cheese layer, then another meat layer. Cover with the rest of the lasagne and the rest of the cheese mixture. Sprinkle the grated cheese on top and cook for 45 minutes or until the top is browned. Serve with garlic bread and a tomato salad.

Moussaka

Serves 5-6

1 lb (400 g) aubergines
1½ lb (600 g) potatoes
Meat sauce
2 onions, chopped
2 cloves garlic, crushed
oil for frying
1 lb (400 g) minced lamb
Italian seasoning
salt and pepper
16-oz (400-g) can tomatoes
3 tablespoons (45 ml) tomato purée
Topping
2 eggs, beaten
8 oz (200 g) natural yoghurt
8 oz (200 g) cheese, grated

Pre-heat the oven to 200°C/400°F/Gas 6. Clean, slice and fry the aubergines. Cook and slice the potatoes. Make up the meat sauce as for the lasagne recipe *(see page 83)*. In a large greased casserole dish put alternate layers of meat sauce and aubergines, starting and finishing with a meat layer. Layer the potatoes on top. Beat together the eggs and yoghurt with half the grated cheese and spread over the potatoes. Sprinkle the remaining cheese on top. Cook for 30-40 minutes or until the top is browned. Serve with garlic bread and a tomato and sweetcorn salad.

Curry
Serves 4-6

This is a student version of chicken dhansak. A word of warning to the uninitiated: if you ever substitute real chillis for chilli powder, be sparing. There is a considerable difference between the two. If you are ever tempted to eat one raw, make sure that you have a large jug of water to hand!

12 oz (300 g) red split lentils
2 cloves garlic, crushed
2 large onions, chopped
2 oz (50 g) butter
1 teaspoon (5 ml) ground ginger
1 tablespoon (15 ml) curry powder *or* 1 teaspoon (5 ml)
    turmeric, 1 teaspoon (5 ml) cumin, 1 teaspoon
    (5 ml) coriander and 1 teaspoon (5 ml) chilli
1 teaspoon (5 ml) chilli
1½ lb (600 g) chicken breasts, boned and cut into small
pieces
8 oz (200 g) potatoes, boiled and diced
16-oz (400-g) can tomatoes
2 oz (50 g) sultanas
1-2 tablespoons (15-30 ml) natural yoghurt
2 tablespoons (30 ml) mango chutney
salt and pepper

Fry the lentils, garlic and onions in the butter. Add the ginger and curry powder (or the four separate spices) and continue to cook for 10 minutes over a low heat. Add the chicken and potatoes and cook for another 5 minutes. Add the tomatoes and sultanas. Add enough water to cover the mixture. Cover and cook until all the water is absorbed (about 20-30 minutes). Add the yoghurt and chutney and season. Mix well. Serve with rice, mango chutney, chopped tomatoes, chopped bananas and cucumber raita *(see page 29)*.

Vegetable goulash

Serves 5-6

This is better if made in advance and re-heated.

> 3 lb (1.25 kg) mixed vegetables, e.g., carrots, courgettes,
>   potatoes, aubergines, mushrooms, corn
> 2 onions, chopped
> 2 cloves garlic, crushed
> oil for frying
> 14-oz (400-g) can tomatoes
> 1 red and 1 green pepper, chopped
> 4 tablespoons (60 ml) tomato purée
> 2 tablespoons (30 ml) paprika
> salt and pepper

Cut the vegetables into bite-sized pieces. Pre-heat the oven to 190°C/375°F/Gas 5. Fry the onion and garlic in a little oil until soft. Mix in the remaining ingredients and transfer to a casserole dish. Cook in the oven for 40 minutes or until all the vegetables are cooked. Serve with sour cream and noodles or rice.

Cod Bake

Serves 4

> 8-oz (200-g) packet frozen chopped spinach
> 4 cod steaks
> oil for frying
> *Sauce*
> 1 oz (25 g) margarine ⎫ *or* 1 packet cheese
> 1 tablespoon wholemeal flour ⎬   sauce mix +
> 12½ fl oz (375 ml) milk ⎪   2 oz (50 g)
> 4 oz (100 g) cheese, grated ⎭   cheese, grated

Pre-heat the oven to 190°C/375°F/Gas 5. Cook the spinach as directed on the packet and put in a casserole dish. Fry the cod for 2-3 minutes on each side and place on top of the spinach. Make the cheese sauce by melting the margarine in a saucepan and blending in the flour. Cook for one minute. Remove from the heat and add the milk slowly, stirring all the time. Return to the heat and bring slowly to the boil, stirring constantly. Add half the cheese and when melted pour the sauce over the cod. Cover with the remaining cheese. Cook for 30 minutes. Serve with new potatoes or potato croquettes.

Cascake

Serves 8-12

This is my version of chocolate fudge cake.

Cake
4 oz (100 g) butter
4 oz (100 g) dark brown sugar
2 eggs, beaten
1 tablespoon (15 ml) cocoa made up to 4 oz (100 g) with
   self-raising flour
1 chocolate flake, crumbled
Fudge icing
1½ oz (40 g) butter
2 oz (50 g) plain chocolate
9 oz (225 g) dark brown sugar
2 teaspoons (10 ml) instant coffee powder
1 tablespoon (15 ml) single cream

Grease a 7-inch cake-tin. Pre-heat the oven to 190°C/375°F/Gas 5. Cream the fat and the sugar together until light and fluffy. Gradually beat the eggs into the fat. Stir in the sifted flour and mix in the chocolate flake. Put mixture into the tin. Bake in the oven for 25-30 minutes or until the cake is well-risen and brown.

Make the fudge icing by melting the butter with the chocolate. Stir in the other ingredients. When the cake is cooked, leave to cool for 5 minutes in the tin then remove to a cooling rack – a clean grill rack will do. Leave to cool for a further 10 minutes. Pour the fudge icing over the cake, covering both the top and the sides. Leave in the refrigerator for at least half an hour before serving. This cake is also good to eat the day after baking when the icing has set a little harder.

Flapjacks
Makes 9-12

4 oz (100 g) butter
4 tablespoons (60 ml) golden syrup
1 tablespoon (15 ml) brown sugar
1 tablespoon (15 ml) raisins
8 oz (200 g) muesli
4 oz (100 g) oats
2 tablespoons (30 ml) brandy (optional)

Pre-heat the oven to 150°C/300°F/Gas 2. Melt the butter, syrup and sugar in a large saucepan. Add all the other ingredients and mix well. Press into a well-greased casserole or roasting dish. Bake for 45 minutes or until the flapjacks are brown and firm to the touch. Remove from the oven, score into squares and leave in the dish to cool for 15 minutes. Serve cold or hot with custard.

Wednesday cakes
Makes 12

I call these Wednesday cakes as this was supposed to be the afternoon devoted to sporting activities. The most exercise these cakes call for is beating up the egg. This is a useful recipe as you do not need any special cake-tins in which to bake them.

8 oz (200 g) wholemeal flour
1 teaspoon (5 ml) baking powder
pinch salt
½ teaspoon (2.5 ml) ginger, *or* other flavouring
4 oz (100 g) butter *or* margarine
3 oz (75 g) brown sugar
2 oz (50 g) raisins
1 egg, beaten
1 tablespoon (15 ml) milk (optional)

Pre-heat the oven to 200°C/400°F/Gas 6. Mix the flour, baking powder, salt and ginger together. Rub the fat into the flour mixture. Mix in the sugar and raisins. Bind together with the egg. If the mixture is too dry add 1 tablespoon (15 ml) milk. Take approximately 1 tablespoon (15 ml) of the mixture and place 12 heaps, spaced well apart, on a greased baking tray. Bake for 15-20 minutes or until firm to the touch.

Cheesecake

Serves 6

> Base
> 2 oz (50 g) butter or margarine
> 4 oz (100 g) chocolate digestive biscuits, crushed
> *Filling*
> 4 oz (100 g) curd cheese
> 2 oz (50 g) cottage cheese
> 4 fl oz (100 ml) natural yoghurt
> 2 eggs, separated
> 1 tablespoon (15 ml) cornflour
> 1 oz (25 g) sugar
> *Topping*
> 5 fl oz (125 ml) sour cream
> 8 oz (200 g) canned fruit pie filling *or* slices of fresh fruit

Grease a 7- or 8-inch loose-bottomed cake-tin. Pre-heat the oven to 180°C/350°F/Gas 4. Melt the butter in a saucepan and add the biscuits. Press the mixture into the bottom of the cake-tin. Chill until hard (approximately 20 minutes). Mix together the cheeses, yoghurt, egg yolks and cornflour. Whisk the egg whites until stiff and fold in the sugar. Fold into the cheese mixture and pour on to the biscuit base. Bake for 30-45 minutes or until firm to touch. Remove from the oven and spread the sour cream over the top. Return to the oven for another 5 minutes. Remove and allow to cool in the tin. When cool remove to a serving plate. Top with the fruit.

Birthday cake

Cake
8 oz (200 g) butter *or* margarine
8 oz (200 g) sugar
4 eggs, beaten
1 oz (25 g) chocolate, melted
8 oz (200 g) self-raising flour
Filling
5 fl oz (150 ml) double cream
2 tablespoons (30 ml) brandy (optional)
16-oz (400-g) can black cherries, strawberries *or* apricots
    (fresh if in season)
Topping
chocolate spread and some flaked almonds *or* 1 tube
    ready-made icing

Grease two 7-inch sandwich-tins. Pre-heat the oven to 190°C/ 375°F/Gas 5. Cream the butter and sugar together until light and fluffy. Beat in the eggs gradually. Beat in the chocolate and gently fold in the flour. Spoon the mixture into the tins, smooth the surface and make a slight indentation in the middle of each tin. (The middle rises more than the sides during cooking.) Bake for 30 minutes. Cool in the tin for 5 minutes, then turn out carefully and leave to cool on a wire tray.

When cool, whip the double cream, adding the brandy if used. Use the cream to cover the top of one of the cakes. Put the fruit on top of the cream. Turn the other cake upside down and decorate the top with the chocolate spread and almonds or icing. Sandwich the decorated cake on top of the fruit and cream.

Carrot loaf

Some people are a little apprehensive about trying this cake. But once they have tried it you can't keep them from it.

8 oz (200 g) wholemeal flour
1 teaspoon (5 ml) ginger
1 teaspoon (5 ml) nutmeg
1 teaspoon (5 ml) baking powder
8 oz (200 g) carrots, peeled and grated
4 oz (100 g) butter *or* margarine
4 oz (100 g) clear honey
4 oz (100 g) brown sugar

Grease a 1 lb loaf-tin. Pre-heat the oven to 170°C/325°F/Gas 3. Mix the flour, spices, baking powder and carrots together. In a saucepan melt the fat, honey and sugar together. Stir into the carrot mixture and mix well. Press into the loaf-tin and cook for 1-1½ hours, until firm to the touch, or until a skewer inserted into the middle of the loaf comes out clean. Remove from the oven and leave to cool in the tin for another 10-15 minutes. Remove carefully. Eat hot or cold, spread with butter.

6 Dinner Parties

The menus in this chapter are designed for those occasions when you are going all out to impress with your culinary expertise. The menus are some of my tried and tested party menus and they have always gone down exceedingly well.

Organizing the shopping is especially important for a successful dinner party. I have been amazed at the number of times I have arrived to eat at friends' houses to find people panicking because something has been forgotten. Once it was the main ingredient. I have arranged this chapter a little differently to avoid such disasters. To make these menus absolutely foolproof, I have devised a shopping list and a time plan for each menu. The shopping list shows you at a glance what ingredients you will need. For the specific quantities, check with the ingredients lists of individual recipes. Once you have followed a couple of these menus, I am sure you will be confident enough to devise your own.

Even if you think you have an ingredient in your store cupboard, do check. It is not uncommon to assume that you have enough of an ingredient only to discover, when the shops are closed, that what you actually have is an empty container.

The menus in this chapter are designed for eight people. You will need lots of cutlery, crockery and sometimes casserole dishes. You will have to beg, borrow or steal these items if you are short of any.

Sometimes you may even have to use other people's ovens. I remember when I was a student that it was not an uncommon sight on Friday and Saturday nights on campus to see students carrying hot dishes from one kitchen to another. Even when I lived off-campus, I once had to use the cooker of some friends who lived further down the road. It was quite funny watching people's faces when the arrival of the pudding was heralded by the front-door bell.

Obviously when you are cooking for larger numbers than you are used to, more time and effort are involved. But by planning your time carefully you will save yourself the fuss and bother of finding you have forgotten something important. Always stay calm – remember, even if something does go wrong that your guests are your friends. Apologize and make a joke of it. The only way you can spoil the evening is by creating a fuss and making people feel uncomfortable. If necessary, drown your sorrows with a few drinks.

N.B. These recipes are also more expensive than most others in this book. If resources allow, a small bottle of liqueur goes down a treat with the coffee. Cointreau is a firm favourite with most people.

Menu 1
Garlic mushrooms on toast
Tarragon chicken
Tagliatelle and courgettes
Orange brûlées
Cheese and crackers
Coffee and liqueurs
Preparation time: 3 hours

Shopping list

1 lb (450 g) mushrooms
oil
butter
4 cloves garlic
salt and pepper
bread
tomatoes and watercress
8 chicken pieces
2 large onions
tarragon
paprika
½ bottle dry white wine

sour cream
tagliatelle
courgettes
4 large oranges
fine dark brown sugar
1 miniature dark run
cheese
crackers
small bottle liqueur
coffee
milk
sugar

Time plan: to eat at 8.30

5.45 Prepare the tarragon chicken.
6.15 Make the orange brûlées.
8.15 Make the garlic mushrooms on toast
8.30 Put on water for tagliatelle and courgettes. Serve starter.
8.35 Cook the tagliatelle and the courgettes.
8.45 Serve the tarragon chicken.

Tarragon chicken
Serves 8

2 large onions, chopped
2 cloves garlic, crushed
3 oz (75 g) butter
8 chicken pieces
½ bottle dry white wine
salt and pepper
2 tablespoons (30 ml) tarragon
10 oz (250 g) sour cream
1 tablespoon (15 ml) paprika

Fry the onion and garlic in 2 oz (50 g) butter until soft. Place in one large or two medium-sized casserole dishes. Fry the chicken in the same pan in 1 oz (25 g) butter. Fry until golden. Pour half the wine over the cooked onion. Season with salt and pepper and lay the chicken pieces on top. Sprinkle with tarragon and pour over the rest of the wine. Cook at 170°C/325°F/Gas 3 for 2½ hours. Add the sour cream just before serving. Serve the dish dusted with paprika.

Orange brûlées
Serves 8

> 4 large oranges
> 3 tablespoons (45 ml) *or* 1 miniature dark rum
> 4 oz (100 g) fine dark brown sugar

Cut the oranges in half. Divide the rum between the oranges and cover each exposed half with the sugar. Grill until the sugar melts and darkens (approximately 5 minutes). Leave for a couple of hours before serving.

Garlic mushrooms on toast
Serves 8

> 1 tablespoon (15 ml) oil
> 5 oz (125 g) butter
> 2 cloves garlic, crushed
> 1 lb (450 g) mushrooms
> 8 slices bread
> tomatoes and watercress for garnish

Heat the oil and butter in a large saucepan. When they begin to froth add the garlic and mushrooms. Cover the pan with a lid and shake at intervals so that the mushrooms are coated in fat. Toast the bread. Serve the mushrooms on the toast, garnished with tomatoes and watercress.

Menu 2
Baked potatoes and caviar
Pork and apricots
Brown rice and peppers
Favourite cheesecake
Cheese and crackers
Coffee and liqueurs
Preparation time: 3 hours

Shopping list

8 small potatoes
sour cream
jar of codfish roe
red pepper
1½ lb (675 g) brown rice
2 lb (800 g) lean pork
canned tomatoes
green pepper
canned apricots
2 packet mixes for pork casserole
1 sachet whipped cream topping

1 packet plain cheesecake mix
packet flaked almonds
1 fresh pineapple, or other fresh fruit
milk
butter
cheese
crackers
small bottle liqueur
coffee
sugar

Time plan: to eat at 8.30
6.05 Make the cheesecake.
6.30 Prepare the pork and apricot casserole.
6.50 Prepare the potatoes for baking.
7.00 Put the potatoes in to cook.
8.10 Add the diced red pepper to brown rice and put on to cook.
8.20 Remove the cooked potatoes from the oven and prepare the starter.
8.30 Serve starter.
8.45 Serve main course.

Favourite cheesecake
Serves 8

> 8 oz (200 g) packet plain cheesecake mix
> 1 sachet whipped cream topping
> 10 fl oz (275 ml) milk
> 1 oz (25 g) flaked almonds
> 2 oz (50 g) butter
> 1 fresh pineapple *or* other fresh fruit

Make up the cheesecake base with the butter. Line a 7-inch flan dish with foil. Press the base mixture into the flan dish. Mix the cheesecake topping from the packet with the whipped cream topping and the milk. Spread the mixture over the base. Sprinkle the almonds on top. Chill in the refrigerator. Cut up the fruit and leave it to chill in the refrigerator. Serve together.

Pork and apricots
Serves 8

> 2 lb (800 g) lean pork
> 2 × 16-oz (400-g) can tomatoes
> 1 green pepper, diced
> 2 packet mixes for pork casserole
> 2 × 16-oz (400-g) can apricots

Make up the sauce mixes as directed on the packets, using the pork, apricots, tomatoes and pepper. Bake at 190°C/375°F/Gas 5 for 2 hours. Serve with brown rice cooked with diced red pepper.

Baked potatoes and caviar
Serves 8

> 8 small potatoes, suitable for baking
> 5 fl oz (125 ml) sour cream
> 4 oz (100 g) jar codfish roe
> black pepper

Scrub and prick the potatoes all over. Bake at 190°C/375°F/Gas 5 for 1 hour 20 minutes. When cooked, roll the potatoes between your hands (this will make the potatoes floury on the inside). Cut large crosses in the top of each potato. Squeeze lightly to open. Mix the codfish roe and sour cream together. Pile the mixture into the cut potatoes. Season with black pepper before serving.

Menu 3
Crudités and mayonnaise
Lamb clementine
Baked potatoes
Baked mushrooms
Chocolate rum mousse
Cheese and crackers
Coffee and liqueurs
Preparation time: 2½ hours.

Shopping list

jar flavoured mayonnaise
selection of vegetables, e.g.,
   celery, carrots and
   cucumber
8 medium-sized potatoes
1 lb (400 g) mushrooms
sour cream
1 packet butter with herbs
   and peppers
8 lamb noisettes, (available at
   large supermarkets)
oil
salt and pepper
1 large onion
3 tomatoes
1 lemon

l large orange
walnuts
bread
butter
8 oz (200 g) plain chocolate
6 eggs
1 miniature dark rum
ginger cake
chocolate flake
cheese
crackers
butter
small bottle liqueur
coffee
milk
sugar

Time plan: to eat at 8.30

6.30 Make the rum mousse.

7.00 Prepare the baked mushrooms by putting a dab of butter on each mushroom. Pile into a greased casserole dish.

7.15 Pre-heat the oven to 220°C/425°F/Gas 7. Prepare the vegetables for the starter.

7.30 Put the potatoes in the oven to bake.

8.00 Start making the lamb clementine.

8.30 Put the mushrooms in the oven to cook. Serve the starter.

8.45 Serve the main course.

Chocolate rum mousse

Serves 8

8 oz (200 g) plain chocolate
6 eggs, separated
4 oz (100 g) butter
ginger cake
3 tablespoons (45 ml) dark rum
1 chocolate flake, crumbled

Melt the chocolate in a bowl over some hot water. Whisk the egg whites and beat the yolks. Melt the butter in the chocolate. Remove from the heat and stir in the yolks. Fold in the egg whites gently. Cut the cake into slices and put in a dessert bowl. Pour the rum over the cake. Cover with the mousse mixture and place in the refrigerator. Sprinkle the chocolate flake on top just before serving.

Crudities

9 oz (225 g) jar flavoured mayonnaise
selection of celery, carrots and cucumber

Top and tail the vegetables and cut into 3-inch (7-cm) lengths. Arrange around a bowl filled with the mayonnaise

Lamb clementine
Serves 8

>8 lamb noisettes
>4 oz (100 g) butter, softened and mixed with
> herbs and peppers
>1 large onion, chopped
>1 lemon
>1 large orange
>3 oz (75 g) walnuts, chopped
>salt and pepper
>8 small slices bread
>3 tomatoes, chopped
>oil for frying

Fry the lamb and onion in the butter for 5 minutes. Grate the rinds from the orange and lemon and extract the juices. Add the zest and juice to the lamb. Add the tomatoes. Cook for a few minutes. Add the walnuts and seasoning. Cover the pan with a lid and allow to simmer for 20 minutes, turning once. Cut circles from the bread and fry in a little oil until both sides are brown. Wrap the bread in foil and keep warm in the oven. Serve each noisette on a circle of fried bread.

Menu 4 (Indian)
Bombay mix
Saag gosht (beef with spinach)
Chicken tikka masala
Mixed vegetable curry
Pilao rice
Ice cream

Preparation time: 1¾ hours
excluding marinating

Shopping list
8 oz (200 g) ghee
oil
4 large onions
garlic
6 oz (150 g) stewing beef
Madras curry powder
tandoori curry powder
cumin
turmeric
allspice
1 lb (400 g) frozen spinach
8 oz (200 g) okra (or whole
    green beans if unavailable)

5 fl oz (125 ml) single cream
packet Bombay mix
natural yoghurt
3 chicken breasts
butter
lemon
8 oz (200 g) potatoes
15-oz (375-g) can tomatoes
1½ lbs (600 g) basmati rice
4 oz (100 g) flaked almonds
4 oz (100 g) sultanas
ice cream
lemon juice

Time plan: to eat at 8.30

Night before: marinate the tandoori chicken.
6.45 Start the saag gosht.
7.00 Soak the pilao rice.
7.15 Put the oven on to heat up.
7.45 Start the chicken tikka masala.
7.50 Start the pilao rice.
8.00 Start the mixed vegetable curry.
8.30 Serve.

Mixed vegetable curry
Serves 6

2 large onions, chopped
2 cloves garlic, crushed or chopped
2 oz (50 g) ghee
1 tablespoon (15 ml) oil
1 tablespoon (15 ml) curry powder
1 tablespoon (15 ml) cumin
8 oz (200 g) okra, trimmed and cut into 1-inch (2.5-cm)
  pieces
8 oz (200 g) potatoes, cut into small chunks
15-oz (375-g) can tomatoes, roughly chopped
10 fl oz (250 ml) water

Fry the onion and garlic in the ghee and oil until soft. Add the curry powder and cumin and fry for 1 minute. Add the okra, potatoes, tomatoes and water. Bring to the boil and simmer for 15 minutes until the potatoes are tender.

Pilao rice
Serves 6

1½ lbs (600 g) basmati rice
1 large onion, chopped
4 oz (100 g) ghee
sprinkling allspice
2 teaspoons (10 ml) turmeric
4 oz (100 g) flaked almonds
4 oz (100 g) sultanas

Soak the rice in cold water for 1 hour. Drain. Fry the onion in ghee until soft, add the seasoning and cook for 1 minute; add the rice and cook for 4 minutes, stirring continuously. Add enough boiling water to come 1 inch (2.5 cm) over the rice. Cover the pan and simmer for 20 minutes or until the water is absorbed. Just before serving, stir in the almonds and sultanas.

Saag gosht (beef with spinach)
Serves 6

    2 oz (50 g) ghee
    2 tablespoons (30 ml) oil
    1 onion, chopped
    2 cloves garlic, crushed or chopped
    6 oz (150 g) stewing beef, cubed
    2 tablespoons (30 ml) Madras curry powder
    1 lb (400 g) frozen spinach, defrosted

Fry the onion and garlic in the ghee and oil until soft. Add the curry powder and cook for 1 minute. Add the rest of the ingredients and mix well. Simmer very gently for 1½ hours.

Chicken tikka masala
Serves 6

    Marinade
    3 tablespoons (45 ml) tandoori curry powder
    3 tablespoons (45 ml) oil
    3 tablespoons (45 ml) lemon juice
    3 tablespoons (45 ml) natural yoghurt

    3 chicken breasts, with skin removed
    2 oz (50 g) butter
    1 teaspoon (5 ml) Madras curry powder
    5 fl oz (125 ml) water
    5 fl oz (125 ml) single cream
    lemon wedges to garnish

Combine the marinade ingredients. Make gashes in the chicken and soak in the marinade overnight. Drain, reserving the marinade. Dot with butter and cook in the oven at 210°C/425°F/Gas 7 for 30 minutes; retain the cooking juices. Fry the curry powder for 1 minute; add the marinade, cooking juices, water and cream. Simmer gently for 10 minutes. Meanwhile, chop the chicken. Serve the chicken with the sauce poured over and garnished with lemon.

Menu 5 (Chinese)
Hot and sour soup
Prawn chow mein
Beef with peppers
Stir-fried vegetables
Boiled rice
Oriental fruit salad

Preparation time: 1 hour

Shopping list

12 oz (300 g) mushrooms
soy sauce
oyster sauce
red wine vinegar
salt and pepper
4 oz (100 g) spring onions
oil
brown sugar
2 red peppers
3 green peppers
2 onions
8 oz (200 g) fresh strawberries
   (optional)

3 kiwi fruit
8 oz (200 g) prawns
12 oz (300 g) stewing beef
flour
sweet chilli sauce
2 oz (50 g) cashew nuts
4 oz (100 g) beansprouts
8 oz (200 g) Chinese noodles
1½ lbs (600 g) rice
butter
12 oz (300 g) canned
   mandarin oranges
12 oz (300 g) canned lychees

Time plan: to eat at 8.30

7.30 Prepare the fruit salad and chill.
7.40 Put the rice on to cook. Put the oven on to heat up.
7.45 Prepare all the vegetables.
8.05 Put the soup on to cook.
8.15 Start the prawn chow mein.
8.25 Start the beef with peppers, then the stir-fried vegetables.
8.30 Serve.

Hot and sour soup
Serves 6

8 oz (200 g) mushrooms, thinly sliced
4 tablespoons (60 ml) soy sauce
1¾ pints (1 litre) water
4 tablespoons (60 ml) red wine vinegar
salt and pepper
4 oz spring onions, finely chopped

Put the mushrooms, soy sauce and water into a large saucepan. Bring to the boil and simmer gently for 15 minutes. Add the vinegar and seasoning and simmer for another 5 minutes. Serve with spring onions sprinkled on top.

Prawn chow mein
Serves 6

8 oz (200 g) Chinese noodles
oil for frying
2 onions, thinly sliced
1 red pepper, sliced
3 tablespoons (45 ml) oyster sauce
8 oz (200 g) prawns

Boil the noodles for 5 minutes, drain and rinse. Fry the onion and pepper until soft, add the oyster sauce and prawns and mix well. Add the noodles to the mixture and heat through.

Beef with peppers
Serves 6

12 oz (300 g) stewing beef, sliced thinly
1 tablespoon (15 ml) flour
oil for frying
2 tablespoons (30 ml) oyster sauce
2 tablespoons (30 ml) sweet chilli sauce
2 green peppers, thinly sliced
2 oz (50 g) cashew nuts

Dust the beef with the flour, then fry for 1 minute, stirring continuously. Turn down the heat and add the rest of the ingredients. Toss together until all the ingredients are coated.

Stir-fried vegetables
Serves 6

> oil for frying
> 4 oz (100 g) beansprouts
> 1 green pepper, thinly sliced
> 1 red pepper, thinly sliced
> 4 oz (100 g) mushrooms, thinly sliced
> 2 tablespoons (30 ml) soy sauce
> 1 tablespoon (15 ml) vinegar
> 1 tablespoon (15 ml) brown sugar

Fry the beansprouts, peppers and mushrooms for 1 minute, stirring continuously. Add the rest of the ingredients. Toss until coated and cook for a further minute.

Boiled rice
Serves 6

> 1½ lbs (600 g) rice
> few knobs of butter

Cook the rice as directed on the packet, then place in a large casserole dish with a few knobs of butter, cover and keep warm in the oven. Before serving fork through thoroughly.

Oriental fruit salad
Serves 6

> 12 oz (300 g) canned mandarin oranges
> 12 oz (300 g) canned lychees
> 3 kiwi fruit, thinly sliced
> 8 oz (200 g) fresh strawberries (optional)

Mix the fruits together. Chill thoroughly.

Menu 6 (Mexican)
Tortilla chips .
Chilli stew
French bread
Avocado salad
Lime and chocolate mousse

Preparation time: 2½ hours

Shopping list

1 bag tortilla chips
sunflower oil
2 onions
garlic
chilli powder
cumin
5 oz (125 g) tomato purée
1 beef stock cube
30 oz (750 g) chilli beans
1 lime
30 oz (750 g) canned
   tomatoes

french bread
brown sugar
1¼ lbs (500 g) stewing beef
   and pork
10 fl oz (250 ml) sour cream
6 oz (150 g) cheese
watercress
lettuce
2 avocados
lemon
10 oz (250 g) plain chocolate
10 oz (250 g) double cream

Time plan: to eat at 8.30

  6.00 Start the chilli stew.
  6.20 Make the mousse. Chill.
  7.15 Make the avocado salad.
  7.45 Cut up the french bread. Grate the cheese.
  8.30 Serve.

Lime and chocolate mousse
Serves 6

> 10 oz (250 g) plain chocolate
> 10 oz (250 g) double cream
> 1 lime, with juice extracted and some of the peel grated

Melt the chocolate in a bowl over some hot water. Whip up the cream until stiff. Add the lime juice to the chocolate and let cool slightly, then add to the cream and mix well. Put into little bowls. Top with some grated lime rind. Chill.

Avocado salad
Serves 6

> 8 oz (200 g) watercress
> 1 lettuce, shredded
> 2 avocados, stoned and thinly sliced
> 1 tablespoon (15 ml) sunflower oil
> 1 tablespoon (15 ml) lemon juice
> 1 teaspoon (5 ml) brown sugar

Mix the salad ingredients together. Combine the oil, lemon juice and sugar and use to dress the salad.

Chilli stew
Serves 6

> oil to fry
> 1¼ lbs (500 g) stewing beef and pork
> 2 onions, chopped
> 10 fl oz (250 ml) water
> 2 cloves garlic, crushed and chopped
> 1 tablespoon (15 ml) chilli powder
> 1 teaspoon (5 ml) cumin
> 5 oz (125 g) tomato purée
> 30 oz (750 g) canned tomatoes, roughly chopped
> beef stock cube, crumbled
> 30 oz (750 g) canned chilli beans

Fry the onion and meat until brown, remove from the heat and add the water; cover and simmer for 1 hour. Mix the rest of the ingredients apart from the beans and add to the meat mixture. Mix well. Simmer for another hour. Add the beans and simmer for 15 minutes.

7 Feeding the Loved One

These menus could more accurately be called seduction suppers. The idea here is to look as if you have not gone to too much trouble. Also, the dishes are designed to look as though you can produce a meal almost instantly! It is best to provide a light sweet, or omit this altogether (liqueur chocolates are always a very acceptable alternative).

Some of these recipes use liqueurs. The cheapest way to get hold of these is to buy a measure from your union bar. But do remember, as I once forgot to do, to take a container in which to bring the drink home.

When cooking a special meal for your loved one, or the person who you hope is to be your loved one, it is worth taking a little trouble over the setting. Do as my boyfriend did. He turned the lights down low, put on soft music and got out the candles. However, I would not follow his example of setting your hair alight by leaning over the candles. The smell of singed hair is not very romantic!

Menu 1
Chicken in seafood sauce
Baby potatoes and green beans
Tipsy fruit salad
Coffee
Preparation time: 30 minutes

Shopping list
2 pieces chicken breast,
  boned
1 packet Cornish seafood
  soup
few mushrooms
can baby new potatoes
4 oz (100 g) packet frozen
  green beans

oil
1 banana
1 apple
1 orange
measure of liqueur
coffee
milk
sugar

Order of cooking
1. Make the fruit salad.
2. Cut the chicken up into
   bite-sized pieces.
3. Put the water on for the
   beans.

4. Make the chicken in
   seafood sauce.
5. Cook the beans and heat
   up the potatoes.

Tipsy fruit salad
Serves 2

    1 orange
    1 apple
    1 banana
    measure of liqueur

Skin the orange and divide into segments. Core and slice the apple. Peel and slice the banana. Arrange the fruit in two bowls and pour over the liqueur. Chill before serving.

Chicken in seafood sauce
Serves 2

    2 pieces chicken breast, boned
    1 small onion, chopped
    oil for frying
    few mushrooms, sliced
    1 packet Cornish seafood soup
    15 fl oz (375 ml) water

Cut the chicken into bite-sized pieces. Fry the onion in the oil until it begins to soften. Add the chicken and fry until golden brown or until the juices from the chicken run clear. Add the mushrooms and cook for a further minute. Meanwhile, make up the soup as directed on the packet using only 15 fl oz (375 ml) water. Pour over the chicken and cook over a low heat for 5 minutes. Serve with the baby new potatoes and green beans.

Menu 2
Pork with apple and cider
Rice with sweetcorn
Honey almond yoghurt
Coffee
Preparation time: 30 minutes

Shopping list

2 pork escalopes (obtainable
   from large supermarkets)
garlic
butter
mushrooms
1 eating apple
cider
salt and pepper
brown rice

8-oz (200-g) can sweetcorn
   and peppers
clear honey
4 fl oz (100 ml) natural
   yoghurt
sliced almonds
coffee
milk
sugar

Order of cooking

1. Put 6 oz (150 g) brown rice
   on to cook.
2. Prepare the Honey almond
   yoghurt.
3. Cook the Pork with apple
   and cider.

4. Heat up the sweetcorn
   with ½ oz (10 g) butter.
5. Mix the cooked rice and
   sweetcorn.

Honey almond yoghurt
Serves 2

    4 fl oz (100 ml) natural yoghurt
    clear honey
    few almonds, sliced

Divide the yoghurt between two bowls and mix in a little honey. Decorate with a few sliced almonds. Chill.

Pork with apple and cider
Serves 2

    1 teaspoon (5 ml) dried rosemary
    1 clove garlic, crushed
    2 pork escalopes
    1 oz (25 g) butter
    few mushrooms, sliced
    ½ eating apple, sliced
    2 fl oz (50 ml) cider
    salt and pepper

Spread the rosemary and garlic over the pork. Fry in the butter for a few minutes on each side until the meat is browned. Drain and put to one side. Add the mushrooms to the pan and fry lightly. Add the apple and cook for a few minutes. Return the pork to the pan and add the cider. Season and simmer gently for 10-15 minutes. Serve on a bed of sweetcorn and rice with the juices from the pan poured over the pork.

Menu 3
Mushroom stroganoff
Buttered tagliatelle
Pears in chocolate sauce
Coffee
Preparation time: 20 minutes

Shopping list
butter
small onion
8 oz (200 g) mushrooms
green pepper
wholemeal flour
red wine
single cream
lemon juice
paprika

soy sauce
salt and pepper
tagliatelle
canned pears
chocolate, preferably plain
honey or golden syrup
coffee
milk
sugar

Order of cooking
1. Put the water on for the tagliatelle.
2. Make the pears in chocolate sauce.
3. Put the tagliatelle on to cook.

4. Make the mushroom stroganoff.
5. Melt 1 ½ oz (35 g) butter and use to coat the tagliatelle.

Pears in chocolate sauce
Serves 2

2 oz (50 g) chocolate, preferably plain
1 tablespoon (15 ml) honey or golden syrup
1 tablespoon (15 ml) cream
few canned pears

Melt the chocolate and honey in a small saucepan over a gentle heat. Remove from the heat and stir in the cream. Mix well. Divide the canned pears between two dishes and pour over the sauce. Leave to cool but do not refrigerate.

Mushroom stroganoff
Serves 2

1½ oz (35 g) butter
1 small onion, chopped
½ green pepper, sliced
8 oz (200 g) mushrooms, sliced
1 tablespoon (15 ml) wholemeal flour
2 tablespoons (30 ml) red wine
4 fl oz (100 ml) single cream mixed with 1 tablespoon
    (15 ml) lemon juice
dash soy sauce
paprika

Fry the onion, pepper and mushrooms in the butter until they begin to soften. Stir in the flour and cook for 1 minute. Season. Add the wine, cream and soy sauce. Simmer gently for 3-4 minutes. Serve on a bed of buttered tagliatelle, dusted with paprika.

8 The Vegetarian Student

When *Grub On A Grant* was first published in 1985 vegetarianism was becoming increasingly popular. Over the past few years this interest in vegetarian cookery has continued to grow. It is generally acknowledged that a vegetarian diet is a healthy way of eating – and a cheaper one too.

With this growth in interest it has become much easier to obtain various items which, when I first wrote *Grub On A Grant*, one could only find in specialist food shops. However, these items are now widely available from supermarkets and therefore I have revised and expanded this section to include recipes which use more beans (some of which could only be bought dried before – but can now be bought cooked in tins) and I have also included recipes which use bulghur wheat and couscous, both of which are now popular alternatives to rice.

You will also notice the use of pesto – this is a mix of basil, pine nuts, garlic, cheese and oil. I love it – and use it to pep up baked potatoes or pasta (lovely lunch dishes) but more importantly a tablespoon of pesto in most dishes really improves the flavour. It is obtained in jars and should be refrigerated when opened – so if sharing a communal student fridge you may wish to substitute dried basil and a little Parmesan cheese where I have used pesto in recipes.

The reasons for the popularity of vegetarianism remain – some abhor the slaughter of animals to feed man, while others object to the way slaughterhouse animals are reared. Many object to the wastefulness of rearing animals or food for animals on land that could be used to grow crops for direct human consumption.

But for many, especially those who are not full-time vegetarians, it is the attraction of a low-fat, high-fibre diet that draws people to vegetarian cookery. This chapter, then, is especially for those who for ethical reasons eat neither meat nor fish. I have not specified vegetarian cheese, although it is now quite widely available – many vegetarians do eat standard cheese – I feel the choice is the individual's and of course you can substitute a vegetarian cheese when I have used cheese in a recipe.

There is also a section at the end of this chapter for use when entertaining vegetarian friends and to this I have added two popular dessert dishes.

Butter beans in cheese sauce
Serves 1

8-oz (200-g) can butter beans
2 tablespoons (30 ml) natural yoghurt
2 oz (50 g) cheese, grated

Heat the butter beans in a small saucepan. Drain. Add the yoghurt to the pan, heat very gently and add the cheese. Continue heating until the cheese melts. Serve with brown rice.

Cheese and lentil pudding
Serves 1

2 oz (50 g) red split lentils
5 fl oz (150 ml) water
2 oz (50 g) cheese, grated
1 small onion, chopped
1 tablespoon (15 ml) tomato purée
salt and pepper
1 egg, beaten

Pre-heat the oven to 190°C/375°F/Gas 5. Cook the lentils in a small saucepan with the water until they form a stiff paste (approximately 10-15 minutes). Remove from the heat and add the cheese, onion and tomato purée. Season. Mix the egg into the mixture, using just enough to bind the mixture together. Grease a one-person casserole dish and press the mixture into it. Bake for 30-35 minutes until golden brown and firm to the touch. Serve with peas and boiled potatoes.

Spiced chick peas
Serves 1

8-oz (200-g) can chick peas
1 teaspoon (5 ml) curry powder *or* garam masala
1 teaspoon (5 ml) tomato purée
1 small onion, chopped and fried in butter
butter for frying

In a saucepan fry the onion in butter until soft. Mix all the ingredients together and heat through. Serve with brown rice.

Curried bean crumble
Serves 1

7-oz (200-g) can baked beans
4 oz (100 g) canned sweetcorn
½ green pepper, diced
1 teaspoon (5 ml) curry powder
1 tablespoon (15 ml) tomato purée
2 slices wholemeal bread, crumbled
1 oz (25 g) cheese, grated

Heat up the beans, corn and pepper in a saucepan. Add the curry powder and tomato purée. Transfer to a flame-proof dish. Mix the breadcrumbs and cheese together and use to cover the dish. Grill until the cheese melts. Serve with toast.

Lentil and potato bake
Serves 1

This is a good recipe to use when introducing non-vegetarian friends to 'veggie' cooking. We even had my boyfriend's Dad – a steadfast meat-eater – asking for more when we cooked this for him.

4 oz (100 g) red split lentils
1 small onion, chopped
oil for frying
6 oz (150 g) potato, cooked and sliced
2 oz (50 g) cheese, grated

Pre-heat the oven to 200°C/400°F/Gas 6. Fry the lentils and onion for 5 minutes or until the onion begins to turn brown. Cover with a little water and cook until the water is absorbed (approximately 10-15 minutes). Spread the lentil mixture in a one-person greased casserole dish. Cover with the potatoes and sprinkle the cheese on top. Bake for 30 minutes. Serve with brown rice.

Ragout of beans
Serves 1

    1 small onion, chopped
    1 carrot, sliced
    oil for frying
    1 tablespoon (15 ml) wholemeal flour
    1 teaspoon (5 ml) vegetable extract
    1 tablespoon (15 ml) tomato purée
    8-oz (200-g) can butter beans
    pinch mixed herbs

Cook the onion and carrot in the oil. Stir in the flour and cook for 1 minute. Add the vegetable extract, tomato purée, beans and herbs. Mix well and cook until the beans are heated through. Serve with toast.

Chick pea kedgeree
Serves 1

    oil for frying
    1 small onion, sliced
    ½ green pepper, sliced
    8-oz (200-g) can chick peas
    1 teaspoon (5 ml) curry powder
    3 oz (75 g) brown rice, cooked
    1 tomato, quartered

Fry the onion and pepper in the oil until soft. Add the chick peas and curry powder. Mix in the rice. Serve garnished with the tomato.

Macaroni hot pot
Serves 1

    1 medium potato, diced
    1 carrot, sliced
    cup vegetable stock
    3 oz (75 g) short-cut macaroni, cooked
    2-3 tablespoons (30-45 ml) condensed tomato soup
    salt and pepper

Cook the potato and carrot in stock until soft (approximately 15 minutes). Add the macaroni and the soup. Season and heat through. Serve immediately.

Piperade
Serves 1

> 1 clove garlic, chopped
> ½ onion, chopped
> oil for frying
> ½ red pepper, chopped
> 1 tomato, chopped
> 2 eggs, beaten
> ground black pepper

Cook the garlic and onion until soft. Add the pepper and tomato. Cook for a few minutes. Add the eggs. Cook, stirring with a fork, until the eggs are lightly scrambled. Season. Serve with toast.

Tomatoes provençale and wholemeal spaghetti
Serves 1

> 3 oz (75 g) wholemeal spaghetti
> 8-oz (200-g) can tomatoes
> few mushrooms
> 1 clove garlic, chopped
> oil for frying

Put the spaghetti on to cook. Drain the tomatoes, reserving half the liquid. Fry the tomatoes, garlic and mushrooms. Add the tomato juice and simmer until the spaghetti is ready. Serve with the sauce poured over the spaghetti.

Undone pie
Serves 1

> 5-oz (125-g) can condensed vegetable soup
> 8-oz (200-g) can sweetcorn
> 1 tablespoon (15 ml) tomato purée
> 1 tomato, sliced
> 2 thick slices french bread
> 2 oz (50 g) cheese, grated

Pre-heat the oven to 200°C/400°F/Gas 6. Mix the soup, corn and purée together. Put the tomato slices into the bottom of a one-person casserole dish. Cover with the soup mix. Put the bread on top and pile the cheese over this. Bake for 20 minutes.

Tomato and pasta bake
Serves 1

    8-oz (200-g) can tomatoes
    3 oz (75 g) short-cut macaroni, cooked
    Italian seasoning
    1 tomato, sliced
    1 slice wholemeal bread
    1 oz (25 g) cheese, grated

Pre-heat the oven to 200°C/400°F/Gas 6. Mix the canned tomatoes, macaroni and seasoning together and put in a greased one-person casserole dish. Layer the tomato slices over. Crumble the bread and mix with cheese. Use to cover the dish. Bake for 25 minutes.

Stuffed aubergine
Serves 1

    1 small aubergine
    1 small onion, finely chopped
    few mushrooms, sliced
    2 oz (50 g) cheese, grated
    1 egg, beaten

Pre-heat the oven to 190°C/375°F/Gas 5. Cut the aubergine in half and scoop out the flesh, leaving a shell. Chop the aubergine flesh and mix with the remaining ingredients. Refill the aubergine shells and bake for 40 minutes. Serve with a tomato salad.

Pasta and creamed mushrooms
Serves 1

    3 oz (75 g) pasta shapes
    1 small onion, chopped
    few mushrooms, sliced
    ½ oz (15 g) butter
    1 tablespoon (15 ml) single cream

Cook the pasta. Fry the onion and mushrooms in butter and mix with the cream. Serve with the pasta.

Tandoori vegetables
Serves 1

> 5 fl oz (125 ml) natural yoghurt
> 2 teaspoons (10 ml) tandoori mix
> squeeze lemon juice
> 1 onion, finely chopped
> 4 oz (100 g) green beans, cooked
> 2 tomatoes, quartered

Mix the yoghurt and tandoori mix with lemon juice. Add the vegetables and leave for 1 hour. Heat gently in a saucepan and serve with rice.

Egg curry
Serves 1

> 3 oz (75 g) brown rice, cooked
> ½ packet curry sauce (check the contents for beef fat)
> 2 eggs, hard-boiled

Make up the curry sauce. Halve the eggs and serve on a bed of rice with the curry sauce poured over.

Wholemeal spaghetti with corn sauce
Serves 1

> 3 oz (75 g) wholemeal spaghetti
> 4-oz (100-g) can sweetcorn
> 1 tablespoon (15 ml) milk
> 2 oz (50 g) curd cheese

Cook the spaghetti. While it is cooking heat the corn, milk and cheese together. Serve the sauce poured over the spaghetti.

Lentil curry
Serves 1

 1 small onion, sliced
 3 oz (75 g) red split lentils
 oil for frying
 1 teaspoon (5 ml) curry powder
 1 tablespoon (15 ml) tomato purée
 8 oz (200 g) mixed diced vegetables

Fry the onion and lentils for 5 minutes. Add just enough water to cover the lentils and cook until water is absorbed (approximately 10-15 minutes). Add the curry powder and tomato purée and mix well. Add the vegetables and enough water to make a sauce. Cover and simmer until the vegetables are cooked (approximately 10-15 minutes). Serve with rice.

Curried lentil pie
Serves 1

 lentil curry mixture (*see above*)
 1 serving instant mashed potato, made up

Pre-heat the oven to 200°C/400°F/Gas 6. Put the lentil mixture into a casserole dish and cover with the mashed potato. Bake for 20 minutes.

Butter bean bake
Serves 1

 8-oz (200-g) can butter beans
 5-oz (125-g) can condensed mushroom soup
 1 slice wholemeal bread
 1 oz (25 g) cheese, grated

Pre-heat the oven to 180°C/350°F/Gas 4. Put the beans and soup into a small casserole dish. Cut the bread into four triangles and cover the beans and soup with them. Sprinkle the cheese on top. Cook for 25 minutes.

Sesame and nut roast
Serves 1

> 1 small onion, finely chopped
> oil for cooking
> stock made with 1 teaspoon (5 ml) vegetable extract
>   dissolved in 2 fl oz (50 ml) hot water
> 2 oz (50 g) brazil nuts, chopped or grated
> 1 oz (25 g) sesame seeds
> 1 slice wholemeal bread, crumbled
> ½ tablespoon (7.5 ml) wholemeal flour
> pinch mixed herbs

Pre-heat oven to 190°C/375°F/Gas 5. Fry the onion in the oil until soft and add the stock. Line a one-person casserole dish with greased foil. Mix with the other ingredients and press into the dish. Bake for 30 minutes or until firm to the touch. Serve with boiled potatoes and tomato ketchup.

Spaghetti and lentils
Serves 1

This is as popular with 'veggie' students as spaghetti bolognese is with the meat-eaters. It might not be an authentic Italian dish, but it always goes down with contented slurps!

> 1 small onion, sliced
> 3 oz (75 g) red split lentils
> oil for frying
> 3 oz (75 g) wholemeal spaghetti
> 1 tablespoon (15 ml) tomato purée
> few mushrooms, finely chopped

Fry the onion and lentils in a little oil for 5 minutes, or until the onion is brown. Add just enough water to cover the lentils and cook until the water is absorbed (approximately 10-15 minutes). Cook the spaghetti. Add the purée and mushrooms to the lentil mixture. Add enough water to make a sauce. Cook for a few minutes. Serve the lentil sauce over the spaghetti.

Rice and bean risotto
Serves 1

3 oz (75 g) brown rice
1 carrot, grated
1 small onion, finely chopped
8-oz (200-g) can kidney beans, drained
soy sauce
½ green pepper, diced

Cook the brown rice. Five minutes before the end of its cooking time place all the other ingredients in the pan on top of the rice. Cover the pan and let the steam from the rice cook the vegetables. When all water has been absorbed, mix thoroughly before serving. Serve with yoghurt flavoured with, for example, mint, tomato purée, lemon juice or curry powder.

Chilli bean goulash
Serves 1

8-oz (200-g) can beans in chilli sauce
½ green pepper, chopped
1 teaspoon (5 ml) paprika
1 tablespoon (15 ml) natural yoghurt

Heat the beans. Add the pepper and paprika and cook for 10 minutes or until the pepper is soft. Serve the beans on a bed of rice or noodles with yoghurt on top.

Nut paella
Serves 1

3 oz (75 g) brown rice
2 oz (50 g) cashew nuts
½ green pepper, diced
4-oz (100-g) can sweetcorn
1 oz (25 g) butter or margarine

Cook the brown rice until all the water has been absorbed. Melt the butter and fry the nuts, pepper and sweetcorn over a low heat for a few minutes. Mix in the rice and stir thoroughly. Serve immediately.

Veggieburgers
Serves 1

This is the vegetarian answer to McDonald's. We served these once when friends came round to celebrate Halloween. That was quite a night! We cut faces out of pumpkins and placed candles inside. Someone put a crash helmet over one of these pumpkin heads, which looked very funny. However, when the helmet was left there it caught fire! Luckily someone noticed it before too much damage was caused.

½ packet vegetarian burger mix
1 egg
1 toasted bap, halved
2 teaspoons (10 ml) relish

Make and cook the veggieburgers as directed on packet (using the egg). Serve a veggieburger on each half of the bap, topped with 1 teaspoon (5 ml) relish. Serve with baked beans or a fried egg.

Brie bake
Serves 1

    1 small onion, chopped
    1 clove garlic, chopped
    oil for frying
    8-oz (200-g) can butter beans, drained ·
    4-oz (100-g) Brie, crust removed
    1 tablespoon (15 ml) pesto
    2-oz (65-g) packet Smash − made up with 10 fl oz (250 ml)
        boiling water and 1 tablespoon (10 ml) soft margarine
    salt and pepper

Fry the onion and garlic in oil until starting to brown. Remove from heat and add beans. Cut Brie into cubes and add with pesto to onion mixture. Put mixture into a one-person greased casserole dish. Cover with the Smash mixture and season with salt and pepper. Bake in a pre-heated oven at 200°C/400°F/Gas 6 for 25 minutes.

Sandwich soufflé
Serves 1

    2 slices wholemeal bread
    1 tablespoon (15 ml) soft margarine
    1 tablespoon (15 ml) chilli or tomato relish
    2 oz (50 g) cheese, grated
    5 fl oz (125 ml) milk
    1 egg, beaten
    salt and pepper

Spread bread with margarine and then chilli or tomato relish. Using half of the cheese, sandwich bread slices together and place in a one-person greased casserole dish. Beat together the milk and egg and season to taste with salt and pepper. Pour this mixture over bread − making sure the bread is fully immersed. Sprinkle with remaining cheese and bake in a pre-heated oven at 200°C/400°F/Gas 6 for 20−25 minutes or until bread is brown and has puffed up.

Peanut stir-fry
Serves 1

1 small onion, chopped
1 clove garlic, chopped
1 carrot, cut into thin matchsticks
1 red pepper, chopped
oil for frying
1 oz (25 g) unsalted peanut kernels
8 oz (200 g) fresh beansprouts
1 tablespoon (15 ml) peanut butter
1 tablespoon (15 ml) honey
1 tablespoon (15 ml) soy sauce
¼ teaspoon (1.25 ml) chilli sauce

Fry onion, garlic, carrot and pepper in oil until starting to brown. Add peanuts and beansprouts and fry for one minute. Mix peanut butter, honey, soy sauce and chilli sauce together and add to the vegetable mixture. Continue to fry until sauce coats vegetables and mixture has heated through. Serve with brown rice.

Cauliflower and bean bake
Serves 1

1 small onion, chopped
1 clove garlic, chopped
oil for frying
3 oz (75 g) soft wholemeal breadcrumbs
1 tablespoon (15 ml) tomato purée
6 oz (150 g) cooked cauliflower, chopped
7-oz (200-g) can baked beans
1 tablespoon (15 ml) pesto
1 oz (25 g) mixed chopped nuts
1 oz (25 g) mozzarella cheese, grated

Cook onion and garlic gently in oil until soft. Turn heat up and add breadcrumbs − continue cooking until browning. Add tomato purée and mix thoroughly. Mix with cauliflower, baked beans and pesto and put in a one-person greased casserole dish. Sprinkle with nuts and then cheese, bake in a pre-heated oven at 200°C/400°F/Gas 6 for 25 minutes.

Avocado and banana with pasta
Serves 1

    3 oz (75 g) pasta
    1 ripe avocado
    1 ripe banana
    1 tablespoon (15 ml) soft margarine
    1 tablespoon (15 ml) smooth peanut butter
    black pepper

Cook pasta in boiling water until *al dente* (soft but still with some bite!). While cooking pasta, peel, stone and chop avocado. Peel and chop banana. Beat together the soft margarine and peanut butter. When pasta is cooked, drain and add other ingredients, seasoning with black pepper. Put back on the heat briefly to heat ingredients through. Serve immediately.

Chick pea curry
Serves 1

    1 small onion, chopped
    1 clove garlic, chopped
    oil for frying
    1-2 teaspoons (5-10 ml) curry powder or paste
    1-2 teaspoons (5-10 ml) tomato purée
    7-oz can (200-g) can chopped tomatoes
    14-oz (400-g) can chick peas, drained
    3 tablespoons (45 ml) Greek yoghurt

Fry onion and garlic in oil until starting to brown. Add curry powder or paste and tomato purée, fry for 1 minute, stirring constantly. Add rest of ingredients and continue to cook until thoroughly heated through. Serve with brown rice, bulghur wheat or couscous.

Broccoli and sweetcorn risotto
Serves 1

1 small onion, chopped
1 clove garlic, chopped
oil for frying
3 oz (75 g) easy-cook rice
6 oz (150 g) broccoli, chopped
15 fl oz (750 ml) vegetable stock
1 tablespoon (15 ml) pesto
4 oz (100 g) canned sweetcorn, drained
sprinkling Parmesan cheese

Fry onion and garlic in oil until soft, add rice and stir-fry quickly. Add broccoli and one-third of the vegetable stock. Simmer gently until the liquid has nearly gone and then add half of remaining vegetable stock; when that too has nearly bubbled away add the pesto, sweetcorn and remaining stock. Stir thoroughly. When liquid has all gone remove from heat quickly before mixture burns. Sprinkle with Parmesan and stir through. Serve with a bottled sauce or chutney.

Pasta and mushrooms with hummus sauce
Serves 1

3 oz (75 g) pasta
1 small onion, chopped
1 clove garlic, chopped
oil for frying
4 oz (100 g) mushrooms, sliced
4 oz (100 g) hummus
1 tablespoon (15 ml) milk
salt and pepper

Put pasta on to cook − it should take 10−12 minutes. Fry onion and garlic in oil until starting to brown. Add mushrooms and continue to cook until soft. Add hummus and milk. Cover and simmer gently for a few minutes. When pasta is cooked, drain and stir sauce into the pasta, season with salt and pepper.

Pasta with peanuts and mushrooms
Serves 1

3 oz (75 g) pasta
1 tablespoon (15 ml) smooth peanut butter
1 tablespoon (15 ml) soft margarine
1 oz (25 g) unsalted peanut kernels
7-oz (200-g) can creamed mushrooms
2 tablespoons (30 ml) milk
black pepper

Cook pasta until *al dente*. While cooking beat together peanut butter and margarine. When pasta is cooked, drain and add rest of ingredients. Season to taste. Return to heat and continue to cook until heated through thoroughly. Serve with Parmesan cheese.

Sweet and sour beans
Serves 1

1 small onion, chopped
1 clove garlic, chopped
1 small green pepper, chopped
oil for frying
14-oz (350-g) can black-eyed beans, drained
6-oz (165-g) jar sweet and sour sauce

Fry onion, garlic and pepper in oil until soft and starting to brown, add black-eyed beans and sauce. Mix thoroughly and continue to heat until mixture is heated through. Serve with brown rice.

Potato and pepper fry
Serves 1

2 small peppers of different colours
1 small onion, chopped
1 clove garlic, chopped
oil to fry
1 medium potato, cut into small cubes
7-oz (200-g) can chopped tomatoes
1 tablespoon (15 ml) pesto

Cut peppers into thin strips approximately 1 inch (2.5 cm) long. Fry peppers, onion and garlic in oil until soft and starting to brown. Add rest of ingredients and mix together. Cover and simmer gently until potato is soft (20–30 minutes). Stir frequently to prevent sticking. Serve with grated cheese and Greek yoghurt.

Sweetcorn and mushrooms with pasta
Serves 1

3 oz (75 g) pasta
1 small onion, chopped
1 clove garlic, chopped
4 oz (100 g) mushrooms, quartered
oil for frying
7-oz (200-g) can chopped tomatoes
7-oz (200-g) can sweetcorn, drained
1 tablespoon (15 ml) tomato purée
1 tablespoon (15 ml) pesto
1 tablespoon (15 ml) chopped mixed nuts

Put pasta on to cook – it should take 10–12 minutes. Fry onion, garlic and mushrooms in oil until soft. Add tomatoes and sweetcorn and simmer gently for 5 minutes. Add rest of ingredients and stir thoroughly. Continue to cook for a few minutes until flavours have infused and mixture is heated throughout. When pasta is cooked, drain and serve with mixture.

Artichoke gratin
Serves 1

- 1 small onion, chopped
- 1 clove garlic, chopped
- oil for frying
- 14-oz (350-g) can artichoke hearts, drained
- 4 oz (100 g) blue Brie, crust removed
- 4 oz (100 g) fromage frais (8%)
- 1 oz (25 g) soft wholemeal breadcrumbs
- 1 oz (25 g) cheese, grated

Fry onion and garlic in oil until soft. Cut each artichoke heart into four and cut blue Brie into small cubes. Mix artichokes, blue Brie, onion, garlic and fromage frais together and put in a one-person casserole dish. Using the pan you fried the onion and garlic in, quickly stir-fry the breadcrumbs. Put on top of ingredients in casserole dish and sprinkle with the grated cheese. Bake in a pre-heated oven at 200°C/400°F/Gas 6 for 30 minutes until golden and bubbling.

Chick peas and pasta
Serves 1

- 3 oz (75 g) pasta
- 1 small onion, chopped
- 2 cloves garlic, chopped
- oil for frying (a good quality oil − olive oil is best)
- 7-oz (200-g) can chick peas, drained

Put pasta on to cook − it should take 10−12 minutes. Meanwhile fry onion and garlic in oil until starting to brown. Add chick peas and a little more oil. Turn heat down and continue cooking until chick peas have heated through. When pasta is cooked, drain, add chick pea mixture and serve immediately.

Stuffed cabbage bake
Serves 1

    4 cabbage leaves (savoy is best)
1 small onion, chopped
1 clove garlic, chopped
oil for frying
2oz (50g) soft wholemeal breadcrumbs
1 tablespoon (15ml) chopped mixed nuts
7-oz (200-g) can chopped tomatoes
2 tablespoons (30ml) Greek yoghurt
1oz (25g) cheese, grated

Prepare cabbage leaves by cutting the hard stalk from each. Fry the onion and garlic in oil until soft and starting to brown. Add breadcrumbs and quickly stir-fry. Remove from heat and mix in nuts. Divide the mixture between the cabbage leaves and wrap loosely. Place folded leaves in a one-person casserole dish, pour tomatoes over leaves and then top with yoghurt and sprinkle with cheese. Bake in a pre-heated oven at 200°C/400°F/Gas 6 for 30–40 minutes until top has browned and is bubbling.

Onion quiche
Serves 1

    1 large onion, sliced
1 clove garlic, chopped
oil for frying
8-oz (200-g) packet shortcrust pastry
4oz (100g) fromage frais (8%)
1 egg, beaten

Fry onion and garlic in oil until soft and starting to colour. While onion is cooking roll out the pastry and line a metal tin. (The bottom of a loaf tin is ideal – bring the pastry just a little up the sides.) Bake in a pre-heated oven at 180°C/350°F/Gas 4 for 10 minutes. Fill with fried onion. Beat together the fromage frais and egg and pour over onion mixture. Bake for another 30–40 minutes. Serve with a green vegetable or salad.

Spicy beans
Serves 1

1 small onion, chopped
1 clove garlic, chopped
1 small pepper, chopped
2 oz (50 g) mushrooms, quartered
oil for frying
1 tablespoon (15 ml) tomato purée
1 teaspoon (5 ml) curry powder or paste
14-oz (400-g) can chilli beans

Fry onion, garlic, pepper and mushrooms in oil until soft. Add rest of ingredients and simmer over a low heat for 5 minutes. Serve with brown rice.

Stuffed courgettes
Serves 1

1 small onion, chopped
1 clove garlic, chopped
oil for frying
2 oz (50 g) bulghur wheat
1 tablespoon (15 ml) raisins
5 fl oz (125 ml) vegetable stock
1 tablespoon (15 ml) pesto
1 tablespoon (15 ml) tomato purée
2 courgettes, halved

Fry the onion and garlic in oil until soft. Add all other ingredients except courgettes. Simmer gently until stock is absorbed and the wheat begins to swell. Scoop out flesh from courgettes, chop flesh and add to mixture, then use this mixture to stuff courgettes. Put in a one-person casserole dish, cover with any left-over mixture and bake in a pre-heated oven at 180°C/350°F/Gas 4 for 30 minutes. Serve with mango chutney and Greek yoghurt.

Bean and tomato soup
Serves 1

1 small onion, chopped
oil for frying
7-oz (200-g) can chopped tomatoes
10 fl oz (250 ml) vegetable stock
1 tablespoon (15 ml) tomato purée
1 tablespoon (15 ml) pesto
7-oz (200-g) can baked beans

Fry onion in oil until soft and starting to colour. Add rest of ingredients and simmer gently for 25 minutes. Stir occasionally to prevent sticking. After 25 minutes, use a wooden spoon to squash some of beans against the side of the pan. Continue cooking for a further 5 minutes, the squashed beans will help to thicken the soup. Serve with French bread and grated cheese.

Stuffed potato bake
Serves 1

1 large potato
1 tablespoon (15 ml) soft margarine
½ teaspoon (2.5 ml) Marmite
salt and pepper
1 hard-boiled egg, finely chopped
2 tablespoons (30 ml) baked beans
2 tablespoons (30 ml) fromage frais (8%)
1 oz (25 g) cheese, grated

Prick the potato all over and bake at 230°C/450°F/Gas 8 for 1–1½ hours or until skin is crispy and inside flesh is soft. Cut potato in half and carefully scoop out potato flesh. Mash with margarine, Marmite, salt and pepper. Spoon back into crispy shells and firm down — making two nests. Mix together chopped egg and baked beans and place in potato nests. Put in a one-person casserole dish and cover with fromage frais and cheese. Turn oven down to 200°C/400°F/Gas 6 and bake for a further 20 minutes.

Spiced vegetable couscous
Serves 1

>   4 oz (100 g) couscous
>   1 small onion, chopped
>   1 clove garlic, chopped
>   oil for frying
>   7-oz (200-g) can chick peas, drained
>   7-oz (200-g) can sweetcorn, drained
>   7-oz (200-g) can chopped tomatoes
>   1 tablespoon (15 ml) tomato purée
>   1 tablespoon (15 ml) pesto
>   1 teaspoon (5 ml) chilli sauce

Soak the couscous in 10 fl oz (250 ml) boiling water — leave until water is absorbed. Meanwhile fry onion and garlic in oil until soft and starting to brown. Add rest of ingredients and mix well. Put couscous in a metal colander (a plastic one will melt) and place over saucepan which contains vegetables. Place a saucepan lid on colander and cook on a low heat for 20 minutes. Serve the spiced vegetable mixture spooned over the couscous.

Cabbage, rice and beans with peanut sauce
Serves 1

>   1 small onion, chopped
>   oil for frying
>   4 oz (100 g) green cabbage, chopped
>   9 oz (225 g) cooked rice
>   7-oz (200-g) can butter beans, drained
>   1 tablespoon (15 ml) peanut butter
>   1 tablespoon (15 ml) soy sauce
>   1 teaspoon (5 ml) chilli sauce
>   8 fl oz (200 ml) vegetable stock

Fry onion in oil until soft and starting to colour, add cabbage and fry for 2 minutes, then add cooked rice and butter beans, mixing thoroughly (you may need to add a little more oil to prevent sticking). Continue to cook until mixture has heated through. Meanwhile put the rest of ingredients in a small pan and heat while stirring. When sauce thickens serve over cabbage mixture.

Beer fondue
Serves 1

> 5 fl oz (125 ml) beer
> 5 oz (125 g) cheese, grated
> 1 clove garlic, chopped
> 1 tablespoon (15 ml) cornflour mixed with
>   a little cold water
> 1 oz (25 g) butter − optional
> ½ teaspoon (2.5 ml) French mustard

Place beer, cheese and garlic in saucepan, heat over gentle heat until cheese is melting. Add cornflour mixture, butter and mustard. Keep stirring while mixture thickens and bubbles. Serve with French bread, which should be dipped into the fondue.

Nut roast
Serves 1−2

> 1 small onion, chopped
> 1 clove garlic, chopped
> ½ oz (12.5 g) butter
> 4 oz (100 g) chopped mixed nuts
> 2 oz (50 g) soft wholemeal breadcrumbs
> 1 teaspoon (5 ml) Marmite
> ½ carrot, grated
> 1 egg, beaten
> sprinkling mixed herbs
> salt and pepper

Fry onion and garlic in butter. When soft and beginning to colour, mix with the rest of ingredients. Put into a greased loaf tin and press down well. Bake in a pre-heated oven at 190°C/375°F/ Gas 5 for 30 minutes. Serve with a bottled sauce or chutney and a green vegetable or salad.

N.B. This is also very good cold, so if you are only cooking for one, save the rest for lunch tomorrow.

Vegetarian dishes for entertaining
All the recipes serve 4-6 people.

Bean paella
Serves 4-5

> 12 oz (300 g) brown rice
> 2 cloves garlic, crushed
> 1 large onion, diced
> oil for frying
> 1 aubergine, diced
> 1 large green pepper, sliced
> 4 oz (100 g) black-eye beans, soaked overnight and boiled
>   for 30 minutes
> 16-oz (400-g) can kidney beans, drained
> 2 large carrots, diced
> few tomatoes, quartered
> 1 teaspoon (5 ml) curry powder
> pinch mixed herbs
> salt and pepper
> 6 oz (150 g) mushrooms, halved

Cook the rice until tender (approximately 20-30 minutes). Fry the garlic and onion in a little oil until soft. Add the aubergine, pepper, beans and carrot and cook for 10 minutes. Stir in the rice, tomatoes, seasoning and mushrooms. Cook gently for 5 minutes. Serve with salad and sour cream or yoghurt.

Barbecued corn-on-the-cob
Serves 4

    4 corn-on-the-cobs
    Sauce
    1 large onion, chopped and fried in butter
    1 tablespoon (15 ml) tomato purée
    1 tablespoon (15 ml) vinegar
    1 tablespoon (15 ml) brown sugar
    dash soy sauce
    1 tablespoon (15 ml) paprika
    1 teaspoon (5 ml) chilli powder

Pre-heat the oven to 200°C/400°F/Gas 6. Boil the corn in plenty of water for 10 minutes. Put all the sauce ingredients in a saucepan. Mix and warm through. When the corn is cooked, cover each one in sauce and put in an individual ovenproof dish. Bake for 30-35 minutes. Serve with baked potatoes and sour cream and a vegetable, such as roast parsnips.

Vegetarian chilli
Serves 5-6

My friend Sue first cooked this for me and since then I have become thoroughly addicted to it. Do, however, remember my earlier warning about substituting fresh chillis for chilli powder!

    1 large onion, chopped
    2 cloves garlic, crushed
    1 aubergine, diced
    1 green pepper, diced
    2 carrots, sliced
    6 oz (150 g) mushrooms, sliced
    32 oz (800 g) canned tomatoes
    oil for frying
    30-oz (860-g) can beans in chilli sauce
    3 tablespoons (45 ml) tomato purée
    1-3 teaspoons (5-15 ml) chilli powder, to taste
    salt and pepper

Fry the vegetables in a little oil until soft. Heat up the beans in a large saucepan and add the vegetables and purée. Season and simmer for 30 minutes. Serve with pittas, sour cream and tortilla chips.

Vegetarian moussaka
Serves 5-6

2 aubergines, sliced
oil for frying
1 large onion, chopped
2 cloves garlic, crushed
16-oz (400-g) can tomatoes
16-oz (400-g) can ratatouille
4 oz (100 g) mushrooms, sliced
Italian seasoning
1½ lb (600 g) potatoes, cooked and sliced
4 eggs, beaten
10 fl oz (250 ml) natural yoghurt
6 oz (150 g) cheese, grated

Fry the aubergine slices on both sides. Drain and put to one side while frying the onions and garlic. When soft, add the tomatoes and ratatouille. Warm through and add the mushrooms and seasoning.

In a large casserole dish layer the aubergine and tomato mixture, starting and finishing with a tomato layer. Cover with the potatoes.

Mix the eggs, yoghurt and half of the cheese together and pour over the potatoes. Sprinkle the rest of the cheese on top. Bake at 200°C/400°F/Gas 6 for 30 minutes. Serve with a salad of tomatoes and corn, with french dressing and garlic bread.

Black-eyed bean fricassée
Serves 4-5

1 large onion, chopped
2 cloves garlic, crushed
2 oz (50 g) butter
4 oz (100 g) mushrooms, sliced
1 tablespoon (15 ml) wholemeal flour
4 tablespoons (60 ml) dry white wine
5 fl oz (150 ml) single cream
10 oz (250 g) black-eye beans, soaked overnight and
  cooked for 30-45 minutes
ground black pepper

Fry the onion and garlic in the butter until soft. Add the mushrooms and fry until cooked. Add the flour and cook for 1 minute. Add the wine, cream and beans. Season. Mix well and heat the beans through. Serve with brown rice.

Nigel's bake
Serves 4

16-oz (400-g) can ratatouille
4 oz (100 g) mushrooms, sliced
2 oz (50 g) almonds, sliced
2 cloves garlic, crushed
2 oz (50 g) butter
2 teaspoons (10 ml) thyme
Topping
1 tablespoon (15 ml) tahini (thinned with dash lemon juice)
1 tablespoon (15 ml) cottage cheese
2 oz (50 g) Cheddar cheese, grated
2 slices wholemeal bread, crumbled

Heat the ratatouille and put in the bottom of a casserole dish. Fry the mushrooms, almonds and garlic in butter until they begin to brown. Put on top of ratatouille and season with thyme.

Mix the topping ingredients together and use to cover the dish. Bake at 220°C/425°F/Gas 7 for 30-40 minutes until the topping is brown and crispy. Serve with brown rice and a vegetable dish.

Provençale flan

Serves 4-6

Flan pastry
4 oz (100 g) wholemeal flour
1 teaspoon (5 ml) baking powder
pinch salt
2 oz (50 g) margarine
1-3 tablespoons (15-45 ml) water
Filling
2 large onions, chopped
1 large red pepper, sliced
2 cloves garlic, crushed
1 oz (25 g) butter
8-oz (200-g) can tomatoes
1 tablespoon (15 ml) tomato purée
pinch mixed herbs
handful pitted black olives

Pre-heat the oven to 180°C/350°F/Gas 4. Make the flan pastry by sieving the flour, baking powder and salt together. Rub in fat until the mixture resembles fine breadcrumbs. Use just enough water to bind into a dough. Roll out to fit a 7-inch flan ring. Weight the pastry down with some coins and 'bake blind' for 10 minutes. While the pastry is cooking make the filling. Fry the onion, garlic and pepper in the butter until soft. Mix in the canned tomatoes and tomato purée. Season and simmer for 10 minutes. Pour the filling into the flan case. Halve the olives and use to decorate the top of the flan. Bake for 30 minutes. Serve hot or cold with various salads and french bread.

Vegetable casserole
Serves 5-6

8-oz (200-g) packet frozen creamed spinach, thawed
2 carrots, sliced
2 courgettes, sliced
1 onion, chopped
6oz (150g) cauliflower
15 fl oz (425 ml) vegetable stock
1 oz (25 g) butter
1 tablespoon (15 ml) milk
pinch herbs
4 oz (100 g) cheese, grated
Topping
1 slice wholemeal bread, crumbled
2 oz (50 g) mixed chopped nuts
2 oz (50 g) cheese, grated
1 teaspoon (5 ml) curry powder or cumin
1 teaspoon (5 ml) paprika

Pre-heat the oven to 200°C/400°F/Gas 6. Cook the spinach as directed on packet. Cook the carrots, courgettes, onion and cauliflower in stock (approximately 10-15 minutes. Drain, reserving 5 fl oz (125 ml) of the stock. Place the vegetables in a casserole dish and put the spinach on top.

Melt the butter, stir in the flour and cook for 1 minute. Gradually add the milk and stock and stir until the sauce thickens. Season. Add the cheese and cook until the cheese melts. Pour the sauce over the casserole.

Mix together the topping ingredients and cover the casserole with them. Bake for 30 minutes. Serve with brown rice.

Mushroom roly-poly

Serves 4-6

Roly-poly pastry
12 oz (300 g) wholemeal flour
pinch salt
2 eggs, beaten
Filling
12 oz (400 g) mushrooms, chopped
6 oz (150 g) cottage cheese
2 eggs, beaten
pinch allspice or nutmeg
Sauce
onion sauce (*see page 53*)
1 tablespoon (15 ml) sherry, vermouth *or* white wine

Sift the flour and salt into a bowl. Make a well in the centre and add the eggs. Mix a well, adding some water if needed to make a soft dough. Chill the pastry while making the filling. (Leave the pastry to rest for at least 30 minutes.)

Mix all the filling ingredients together. Roll out the chilled dough to a thin rectangle and spread with the filling, leaving a good margin on all edges. Roll up like a swiss roll and wrap in well-greased foil. Steam over a large saucepan for 2 hours. Remember to check the water level in the saucepan during cooking. Unwrap and cut into slices.

Make up the onion sauce, adding the sherry. Serve the roly-poly in slices with the suace poured on top. Accompany with roast potatoes and a green vegetable.

Party pancakes
Serves 4-6

Pancakes can be served at a dinner party in a variety of ways. They can be made a little while in advance and kept warm in the oven, separated by greased foil, until it is time to serve them. They make an attractive feature if you fold them in half and then half again, so that a cornet-shape is formed which can be stuffed with your chosen filling. A 'cake' of flat pancakes can be made with different fillings between the layers, which then has a sauce poured over it and is baked.

The other way of baking pancakes in a sauce is to make your familiar rolled pancakes, with chosen fillings inside, then place them in a casserole dish with a sauce poured over. Whatever way they are cooked pancakes are delicious with crusty bread or rice and a salad.

Suggested sauces:

> Cheese sauces (*see page 86*)
> Onion sauce (*see page 53*)
> Packet soup made with half stated quantity of water

If you use a packet soup or sauce mix, remember to check the packet for animal products used in their manufacture.

Pancake mixture
Makes 12 pancakes

> 6 oz (150 g) wholemeal or buckwheat flour
> pinch salt
> 1 egg, beaten
> 15 fl oz (425 ml) milk
> 1 teaspoon (5 ml) oil

Sift the flour and salt into a bowl. Make a well in the middle and fill with the beaten egg and half the milk. Beat together well, gradually adding more milk until a thin batter is formed. Mix in the oil.

Heat a little oil in a frying-pan and cook 2 tablespoons (50 ml) of the mixture for 2-3 minutes. Flip the pancake over and cook the other side for a minute or two.

Fillings

Below are given some suggestions for pancake fillings with an international flavour. The quantities given are enough to fill one pancake.

Italian: 1 tablespoon (15 ml) curd cheese, pinch basil, chopped spring onions

Spanish: 1 chopped onion, 1 chopped tomato, pepper and oregano

Mexican: 1 tablespoon (15 ml) tomato purée, 1 teaspoon (5 ml) chilli powder, 1 tablespoon (15 ml) sweetcorn

Chinese: sauté some beansprouts in butter, add soy sauce, sliced mushrooms and ground ginger

Swiss: grated gruyère cheese, 1 tablespoon (15 ml) cream, freshly milled black pepper

French: chopped mushrooms fried with garlic with 1 tablespoon (15 ml) cream

Indian: 3 tablespoons (45 ml) natural yoghurt, diced cooked potato, 1 teaspoon (5 ml) curry powder, squeeze lemon juice

British: cooked spinach, 1 tablespoon (15 ml) cream, mustard

Three-veg feast
Serves 4-6

These three vegetable dishes can be served together as a complete meal or separately as a vegetable accompaniment.

Cauliflower cheese almond

1 large cauliflower
3 oz (75 g) cheese, grated
2 oz (50 g) almonds, flaked

Divide the cauliflower into florets and cook in boiling water for 8-10 minutes. Put in a flame-proof dish and cover with the grated cheese and flaked almonds. Grill until the cheese melts and the almonds turn brown. Watch carefully as almonds burn easily.

Green beans and basil

8-12 oz (200-300 g) frozen green beans
2 teaspoons (10-15 ml) basil
2 oz (50 g) butter
garlic (optional)

Cook the frozen green beans as directed on the packet. Fry a little basil in the melted butter, adding some crushed garlic if not present in any other part of the meal. When the beans are cooked, drain and add to butter. Shake the pan and cover the beans in butter and basil. Serve hot.

Glazed turnips

1 lb (400 g) turnips
2 oz (50 g) butter
1-2 tablespoons (15-30 ml) brown sugar
1 tablespoon (15 ml) vegetable stock or water

Peel and slice the turnips. Fry in the butter until they soften and begin to brown. Add the brown sugar and liquid. Increase the heat until the liquid evaporates and the turnips are glazed. Serve hot.

Banoffee pie
Serves 4−6

> 10 oz (250 g) butter
> 8 oz (200 g) plain chocolate digestive biscuits
> 16-oz (400-g) can condensed milk
> 2 bananas, sliced
> 5 fl oz (125 ml) whipping cream

Melt 4 oz (100 g) of butter and break biscuits into crumbs. Mix butter and biscuits together. Line a 7-inch flan tin with foil and then press mixture into base of tin − bringing it a little up sides of tin. Melt rest of butter and add canned milk. Bring to boil, then simmer for 5 minutes. Put half of bananas in flan case. When butter and milk mixture has cooled, beat well and then spread over bananas. Chill. To serve, whip cream and use to top flan mixture, then decorate with remaining banana slices.

Apple filo pie
Serves 4−6

> 2 lb (800 g) Cox's apples, peeled, cored and sliced
> 4 oz (100 g) raisins
> sprinkling cinnamon
> 1 tablespoon dark brown sugar
> 10 oz (250 g) filo pastry
> melted butter
> 1 egg yolk, beaten

Mix sliced apples, raisins, cinnamon and sugar together. Grease a deep 7-inch cheesecake dish (with removable bottom), then line with pastry sheets which have been brushed with melted butter. Save some pastry to cover top. Fill dish with apple mixture and then cover with pastry. Bring any overlapping pastry up over the top of pie so that filling is entirely covered. Brush with egg yolk and bake for 45 minutes at 180°C/350°F/Gas 4. After 20 minutes cover with foil to prevent burning.

9 The Slimming Student

Most students can skip this chapter quite happily but, if that day comes when you do not like what you see in the mirror, act immediately. The problem will only get worse.

These diets are for people who are only a little overweight – up to one stone. If you are drastically overweight you would be wiser to seek your doctor's help. The diets given are both cheap and effective. However, as usual, the most effective element of any diet is willpower.

Four diets are given here. Three are one-week diets, including one for drinkers, and another is a crash diet. This should only be followed for three days.

Medical opinion is opposed to crash diets as not only can they be unsafe if followed for too long a time but they are now also suspected as being a cause of obesity. Crash diets are useful in as far as you can successfully lose a few pounds very quickly; for a special occasion when you want to fit into clothes you cannot normally wear because you have become overweight. However, weight lost on crash diets always returns quickly as it is not a loss of fat but glycogen and water. Glycogen is a muscle sugar which is stored in the body for use as instant energy. One of the problems with crash dieting is that by using your body's supply of glycogen, you trigger off hunger pangs which will lead to weakness and depression, and sometimes dizziness and fainting attacks.

Why are medical experts suspicious that dieting can actually lead to obesity? The answer is that it has been found that when on a diet if your calorie intake falls below a certain level your body reacts to the shortage by trying to store some of the food as fat – in preparation for the famine it thinks it is experiencing. Your metabolic rate becomes slower, so your body burns up calories so that you need to consume even less calories to stay the same weight.

If you really want to lose weight you must do so gradually over a long period. This is the only way to lose your fatty deposits. So even though you can lose 5 pounds on the crash diet and only 1½-2 pounds on the other diets, it is wisest to diet slowly as you have more chance of the weight staying off.

The amount of weight that you lose is also dependent on how much exercise you take. Medical experts have swung back to recommending that exercise is a crucial factor in losing weight. You should try to be more active generally. Try to indulge in some sports weekly. Two or three sessions of badminton, squash or some other really active exercise will do wonders for your fitness level. Remember, however, that just standing around on a court won't make any difference – you actually have to make an effort while you are exercising. If you do not work up a sweat and get that nice warm feeling of fatigue after exercising – you are not stretching yourself.

Men are luckier than women in respect to dieting in that they require more calories to maintain a steady weight and can lose weight on a higher daily calorie intake than a woman. Men following these diets can safely add up to 400 calories a day and still lose weight. I would advise that the extra calories consumed come from high fibre food. Most average slices of bread supply 100 calories as do 1 oz (25 g) dry weight of rice or pasta. It would be better to take your extra calorie allowance in one of these forms rather than to have it as an extra 2 pints of lager!

So the ingredients for a successful diet are some exercise, moderation in your calorie intake and a lot of willpower. It's up to you!

Three-day crash diet
(Approximately 500 calories per day)

DRINKS – black coffee or tea, slimline drinks (all in moderate quantities)

DAY 1

Breakfast
1 diet yoghurt
2 crispbreads spread with
  yeast extract

Lunch
1 boiled egg
2 crispbreads spread with
  yeast extract
1 apple

Dinner
small carton of cottage
  cheese
salad made from: lettuce,
  cucumber, celery,
  mushrooms
2 crispbreads spread with
  yeast extract
1 apple

DAY 2

Breakfast
1 boiled egg
2 crispbreads spread with
  yeast extract

Lunch
1 slimming vegetable soup
2 crispbreads
1 apple

Dinner
1 grapefruit
2 oz (50 g) lean ham
salad as Day 1
1 diet yoghurt

DAY 3

Breakfast
1 grapefruit

Lunch
small carton cottage cheese
2 crispbreads
1 apple

Dinner
1-egg omelette with 2 oz
  (50 g) lean ham
salad as Day 1

BURP!

Summer diet
(Approximately 1000 calories per day)

DRINKS — black coffee or tea (or use milk from allowance) slimline drinks. NO ALCOHOL.

ALLOWANCES — ½ pint (250 ml) skimmed milk daily
*Recipes given on p.147.

Breakfast

1 diet yoghurt
1 boiled egg
2 crispbreads spread with
  yeast extract

1 oz (25 g) cereal
5 fl oz (150 ml) skimmed milk
2 crispbreads spread with
  yeast extract

2 oz (50 g) lean ham
1 small fried or poached egg
1 medium tomato

Lunch

2 oz (50 g) lean ham
1 grapefruit
2 crispbreads spread with
  yeast extract
1 apple

5 oz (150 g) cottage cheese
3 crispbreads

1 camembert portion
2 crispbreads
a few grapes

Dinner

6 oz (150 g) cold roast
  chicken
3 oz (75 g) peas or carrots
6 oz (150 g) boiled new
  potatoes

1 packet ready-made chilli
  con carne
1 diet yoghurt

Ham and pasta salad*
1 diet yoghurt

1 regular hamburger
1 small portion french fries
1 diet cola

Super salad*
1 diet yoghurt

1 grapefruit
courgette and ham au gratin*
1 diet yoghurt

2-egg cheese omelette
— made with 2 eggs, 2 oz
  (50 g) grated cheshire
  cheese, dab margarine
salad — lettuce, cucumber
  and 2 tomatoes
1 diet yoghurt

Recipes

Ham and pasta salad

    2 oz (50 g) pasta shapes, cooked
    2 oz (50 g) lean ham, chopped
    6-oz (150-g) can pineapple (in its own juice), chopped
    1 tablespoon (15 ml) natural yoghurt flavoured with lemon
        juice

Mix all the ingredients together and serve.

Super salad

    5 oz (150 g) cottage cheese
    1 tablespoon (15 ml) roast peanuts
    3 oz (75 g) red cabbage, shredded
    4 oz (100 g) canned sweetcorn, drained
    ½ onion, chopped
    1 carrot, grated

Mix all the ingredients together and serve.

Courgettes and ham au gratin

    2 small courgettes, topped and tailed
    2 slices lean ham
    3 tablespoons (45 ml) natural yoghurt
    2 oz (50 g) cheshire cheese, grated
    pinch mustard powder

Boil the courgettes whole for 8-10 minutes. Wrap a slice of ham
around each one and place in an ovenproof dish. Mix the
cheese, yoghurt and mustard powder. Season and pour over the
courgettes. Bake at 200°C/400°F/Gas 6 for 20 minutes.

Winter diet
(Approximately 1100 calories per day)

DRINKS: as for summer diet
ALLOWANCES: as for summer diet
*Recipes given on p.149-50.

Breakfast

As for summer diet

Lunch

1 low-calorie soup
1 wholemeal roll
1 apple

7-oz (200-g) can baked
  beans
1 small slice wholemeal
  bread, toasted

Toasted sandwich
Make a sandwich with 2 small slices wholemeal bread and 1 slice processed cheese. Toast bread on both sides of sandwich so that cheese inside melts.

Dinners

4 grilled fish fingers
2 grilled tomatoes
½ can green beans
2 oz (50 g) rice

2 grilled beef sausages
7 oz (200 g) tin baked beans
1 wholemeal roll

small chicken pie
½ × 8-oz (200-g) can
  sweetcorn
½ × 16-oz (400-g) can green
  beans
1 diet yoghurt
1 small can lager

1 cod in sauce
2 oz (50 g) rice
½ × 8-oz (200-g) can
  sweetcorn
1 diet yoghurt

Beef cobbler*
1 diet yoghurt

Lamb pilaff*
1 diet yoghurt

Quick carrot curry*
2 oz (50 g) rice, cooked
1 apple
1 small can lager

Recipes

Beef cobbler

    4 oz (100 g) beef, minced
    1 small onion, chopped
    ½ tablespoon (7.5 ml) wholemeal flour
    8-oz (200-g) can tomatoes
    1 tablespoon (15 ml) tomato purée
    few mushrooms, sliced
    pinch mixed herbs
    salt and pepper
    Topping
    1 slice wholemeal bread spread with ½ oz (15 g)
        low-cal margarine

Pre-heat oven to 200°C/400°F/Gas 6. Fry the beef and onion until the meat is browned. Remove excess fat from the pan. Add the flour and cook for 1 minute. Add the remaining ingredients and cook for 10 minutes and turn into an ovenproof dish. Cut the bread into 4 triangles and arrange over the beef 'buttered' side up. Bake for 15-20 minutes until the topping is crisp.

Lamb pilaff

    2 lean lamb chops, grilled
    2 tablespoons (30 ml) yoghurt flavoured with curry powder
        and tomato purée
    2 oz (50 g) brown rice, cooked

Cut the lamb from the bone. Mix with the flavoured yoghurt and serve over the rice.

Quick carrot curry

2 carrots
1 small onion, chopped
½ green pepper, sliced
4 tablespoons (60 ml) orange juice + 6 tablespoons
  (90 ml) water
5 oz (125 g) natural yoghurt flavoured with curry
  powder and tomato purée

Clean, top and tail the carrots. Cut into thin 3-inch lengths and boil with the onion and green pepper in the orange and water mixture for 5-8 minutes until cooked. Add more liquid during cooking if needed. When the carrots are cooked add the flavoured yoghurt and heat gently to warm the sauce through. Serve with 2 oz (50 g) cooked rice.

The drinker's diet
(Approximately 1200 calories per day)

ALLOWANCES
½ pint (250 ml) skimmed milk daily
½ oz (15 g) low-fat margarine

DRINKS
black tea or coffee *or* use milk from allowance
slimline drinks plus 3 drinks from allowed list daily.

Allowed drinks:

> 1 glass wine
> ½ pint lager, not extra strong or pils
> ⅓ gill dry vermouth
> ⅙ gill gin
> ⅙ gill whisky
> ⅙ gill vodka

(Half a pint of cider or beer can be taken but must be counted as two drinks per ½ pint. A standard pub measure is ⅙ gill.)

Breakfast

1 oz (25 g) cornflakes,
branflakes or frosties taken
with milk from allowance

Lunch

2 DAYS
sandwich made with 2 slices
ham, 2 small slices wholemeal
bread, sliced tomato

3 DAYS
sandwich made from 1 oz
(25 g) liver and bacon pâté, 2
small slices wholemeal bread,
sliced tomato

1 DAY
chocolate bar

1 DAY
1 packet crisps and drink from
allowance

Dinner

2 beef sausages, grilled
2 oz (50 g) mushrooms,
 grilled
1 tomato
1 apple

6 oz (150 g) roast chicken
6 oz (150 g) baked potato
4 oz (100 g) low-cal coleslaw

2 fishcakes, grilled
2 oz (50 g) mushrooms,
 grilled
7-oz (200-g) can baked
 beans
2 potato croquettes, baked

1 cod-in-sauce
2 oz (50 g) mushrooms,
 grilled
3 potato croquettes, baked

3 oz (75 g) spaghetti
margarine from allowance
½ oz (15 g) Cheshire cheese,
 grated

3 oz (75 g) spaghetti
margarine from allowance
2 slices lean ham, chopped
2 oz (50 g) mushrooms, sliced

2 egg omelette
2 slices lean ham, chopped
4 oz (100 g) low-cal coleslaw

10 Lifesavers

At some time in your student career the day will dawn when term is coming to an end and also your overdraft facility. Now is the time to tighten your belt and make the effort to keep body and soul together while looking forward to getting back to the luxury of home-cooking.

These last recipes are extremely cheap – but often fattening and lacking in temptation. On the other hand they are filling and do allow you to spend your last few pennies on the more important things in life, that is, drink! If you do have any spare pennies, however, you will be surprised at what you can make from these cheap basic recipes. Pizza especially is a firm favourite when you can afford to spend money on more exotic toppings.

Spaghetti

4 oz (100 g) wholemeal spaghetti
margarine
black pepper
Italian seasoning

Cook the spaghetti, drain and add a knob of margarine. Season and serve. Spare cash can be used to buy cheese or sauces to serve with the spaghetti. Canned fish in tomato sauce can be mashed and used as a fishy sauce.

Baked potatoes

1-2 potatoes, cleaned
margarine
salt and pepper

Cook the potatoes at 220°C/425°F/Gas 7, with skewers pushed through them or pricked well all over, for 1-1½ hours. Cut in half and fork in margarine. Grated or cottage cheese can be put on top or baked beans if finances can stretch to such luxuries!

Rice and potatoes

8 oz (200 g) potatoes
4 oz (100 g) rice
oil for frying
soy sauce

Dice the potatoes and fry while cooking the rice. Add a dash of soy sauce to the potatoes while cooking. Serve potatoes on a bed of rice. Any other cheap vegetables can be fried and added.

The following recipes show you what can be done with the very basics — flour, milk, eggs and oil.

Individual Yorkshire pudding

2 oz (50 g) flour
pinch salt
1 egg, beaten
5 fl oz (150 ml) milk

Sift the flour and salt together. Make a well in the middle and pour in the egg and half of the milk. Combine and beat to a thick batter. Gradually add the rest of the milk to make a smooth batter. Grease well a one-person casserole dish and pour in the batter. Cook at 200°C/400°F/Gas 6 for 30-35 minutes or until the batter is brown and well-risen. Serve with gravy, or fried onions if available.

Quick pizza

Base
4 oz (100 g) wholemeal flour
1 teaspoon (15 ml) baking powder
pinch salt
3 fl oz (75 ml) milk
Topping
2-3 tablespoons (30-45 ml) tomato purée
pinch mixed herbs or Italian seasoning
2 oz (50 g) cheese, grated

Grease a baking tray and pre-heat the oven to 220°C/425°F/Gas 7. Mix the base ingredients to a stiff dough. Roll out to a round and place on the baking tray. Cover with tomato purée and herbs. Sprinkle the cheese on top. Bake for 20-25 minutes until the base has thickened and the cheese is bubbling. Vegetables can be fried and put on the pizza base before covering with cheese.

Fritters

2 oz (50 g) flour
pinch salt
1 egg, beaten
2 fl oz (50 ml) milk
oil for frying
Seasoning
1 tablespoon (15 ml) sweetcorn *or* 1 small apple, diced *or*
pepperami, cold and diced

Sift the flour and salt into a bowl. Make a well in the centre and add the egg and half the milk. Mix into the flour gradually and beat in the rest of the milk. Mix in the chosen seasoning. Heat the oil in a frying pan. Put 2-3 tablespoons of mixture in the pan and fry for 2-3 minutes on each side. Serve with tomato ketchup. Makes 2-3 fritters.

Pancakes

2 oz (50 g) wholemeal flour
pinch salt
1 egg, beaten
5 fl oz (150 ml) milk
1 teaspoon (15 ml) oil
oil for frying
Fillings
chopped mushrooms and curd cheese *or* chopped onion and grated cheese *or* any fried vegetable and tomato purée *or* lemon and sugar

Make up the batter as for Yorkshire pudding (*see page 157*) adding 1 teaspoon oil to final batter. Heat a little oil in a frying pan. Add 2 tablespoons to the pan, running the batter over the bottom of the pan. Cook for 2-3 minutes then flip over and cook for a minute or two on the other side. Fill with chosen filling. Serve hot. Makes 3 pancakes.

11 Versatile Slow-cooking

If you haven't got a slow-cooker I strongly advise you to beg, borrow or steal one – or as a last resort buy one out of your next grant cheque! They are only about £15–£20 for a one-person cooker, are extremely easy to cook with and can save you a fair amount of money because the meals you create with them do not require expensive cuts of meat or other pricey ingredients.

Cooking with a slow-cooker usually means that very little preparation is involved. Generally it is just a case of putting the food in it and turning it on. Then, magically, when you return from a hard day's lectures you will have a tasty (and cheap) meal awaiting you. And if by chance you should get back rather later than you'd intended, perhaps after stopping off for a drink, you'll find no cause for alarm: it is virtually impossible to ruin a meal in a slow-cooker by over-cooking because the heat is so low. Another plus-point is returning to a highly appetizing smell; and when you've eaten your delicious slow-cooked meal, you've only got the slow-cooker and your plate to wash up.

Don't be concerned about bumping up your electricity bill because you are leaving your slow-cooker on all day: they use about as much electricity as the average light bulb, so you won't notice any difference.

I would advise you to keep your slow-cooker in your room whether it is in use or not. Why? First, when not in use it is a prime target for thieves, and secondly, when in use it is a prime target for jokers who think that it is a lark to add other ingredients, so that a medium curry, for example, becomes a ferocious chilli-hot curry. I never used my slow-cooker in the college kitchen because I suspected that what came out would have little to do with what had originally gone in. Also, if during cooking the lid is repeatedly lifted off (to see what is cooking inside – people can be very nosy) it slows the cooking time down. So make sure that you use it in your room.

Even the most inexperienced cook (yes, even those who

have never boiled an egg) can produce very edible dishes in a slow-cooker. These recipes are for one person only but most slow-cookers an accommodate enough for two – all you have to do is double the quantities.

One word of warning – don't forget to turn your slow-cooker *on* in the morning before you leave for lectures. It is very sad to return at the end of the day expecting a good nosh-up to find a cold and inedible mixture awaiting you.

Soups

One of the things that slow-cookers are extremely good at is producing beautiful, cheap soups. You will find those that follow tasty, filling and very, very cheap (very useful when funds are running low towards the end of term). Serve these soups with plenty of chunky bread to mop up every last delicious drop of soup.

Potato and garlic soup
Serves 1

> 1 small onion, chopped
> 8 oz (200 g) potato, finely chopped
> 2 cloves garlic, crushed or chopped
> 10 fl oz (250 ml) hot chicken stock
> 1 tablespoon (15 ml) flour

Put all the ingredients apart from the flour into the slow-cooker. Cook for 8–10 hours. Blend flour with a little water and add to the cooker about 30 minutes before you wish to serve the soup.

Tomato and vegetable soup
Serves 1

> 15-oz (375-g) can tomatoes, roughly chopped
> 8 oz (200 g) mixed root vegetables, peeled and chopped
> sprinkling of mixed herbs
> dash of worcester sauce

Put all the ingredients into the slow-cooker. Cook for 7-9 hours.

French onion soup

Serves 1

8 oz (200 g) onion, chopped
1 teaspoon (5 ml) brown sugar
10 fl oz (250 ml) hot brown stock
1 tablespoon (15 ml) flour
2 slices toasted french bread
1 oz (25 g) grated cheese

Put the onion, sugar and stock into the slow-cooker. Cook for 6-8 hours. Thirty minutes before serving blend the flour with a little water and add to the cooker. Serve with the toast and the cheese floating on top of the soup.

Chilli soup

Serves 1

7-oz (175-g) can tomatoes, roughly chopped
1 teaspoon (5 ml) chilli powder
8 oz (200 g) carrot, grated
small onion, chopped
1 tablespoon (15 ml) tomato purée
5 fl oz (125 ml) water

Put all the ingredients into the slow-cooker. Cook for 6-8 hours.

Rich mushroom soup

Serves 1

1 onion, chopped
6 oz (150 g) mushrooms, chopped
10 fl oz (250 ml) brown stock
sprinkling mixed herbs
couple dashes worcester sauce
1 tablespoon (15 ml) tomato purée
1 tablespoon (15 ml) flour

Put all the ingredients apart from the flour into the slow-cooker. Cook for 7-8 hours. Thirty minutes before serving blend the flour with a little water and add to the cooker.

Curried lentil soup
Serves 1

    3 oz (75 g) red lentils
    1 small onion, chopped
    2 carrots, peeled and chopped
    1 medium potato, peeled and chopped
    1 tablespoon (15 ml) tomato purée
    1 teaspoon (5 ml) mild curry powder
    1 teaspoon (5 ml) cumin
    13 fl oz (325 ml) hot stock

Put all the ingredients into the slow-cooker. Cook for 8-10 hours.

Main-course dishes

Oriental vegetables
Serves 1

    1 small green pepper, sliced thinly
    1 small onion, sliced
    4 oz (100 g) carrots, thinly sliced
    4 oz (100 g) parsnips, thinly sliced
    1 tablespoon (15 ml) brown sugar
    1 tablespoon (15 ml) soy sauce
    1 tablespoon (15 ml) tomato purée
    5 fl oz (125 ml) pineapple or orange juice
    1 tablespoon (15 ml) flour

Put all the ingredients apart from the flour into the slow-cooker. Cook for 8-10 hours. Blend the flour with a little water and add to the cooker about 30 minutes before you wish to serve. Serve with brown rice.

Indonesian chicken

Serves 1

    1 small onion, chopped
    1 small green pepper, chopped
    8-oz (200-g) portion chicken, with skin removed
    7-oz (175-g) can sweetcorn
    1 small banana, chopped
    1 teaspoon (5 ml) mixed herbs
    1 teaspoon (5 ml) peanut butter
    5 fl oz (125 ml) chicken stock

Put the onion and pepper into the slow-cooker, put the chicken on top of the vegetables, add the corn and banana and sprinkle the herbs over the top. Dissolve the peanut butter in the hot stock and pour into the cooker. Cook for 6-8 hours. Serve with a green vegetable and rice or pasta.

Goulash

Serves 1

    8 oz (200 g) stewing beef, cut into cubes
    1 small onion, chopped
    1 small green pepper, finely sliced
    2 teaspoons (10 ml) paprika
    1 tablespoon (15 ml) tomato purée
    7-oz (175-g) can tomatoes, roughly chopped
    2 tablespoons (30 ml) sour cream or natural yoghurt

Put the beef, onion and pepper into the slow-cooker; mix the paprika, purée and tomatoes together and pour over the meat. Cook for 8-10 hours. Just before serving mix in the sour cream or yoghurt. Serve with noodles or rice.

Herby meatballs
Serves 1

8 oz (200 g) minced beef
4 oz (100 g) sausagemeat
1 small onion, finely chopped
Italian seasoning
a little beaten egg
salt and pepper
5-oz (125-g) can condensed tomato soup

Combine all the ingredients apart from the soup, using just enough egg to bind them together. Divide into 6 portions and roll each portion into a ball. Put the balls into the slow-cooker and pour the soup over them. Cook for 4-6 hours. Serve with noodles or rice. (Sometimes the meatballs break up when you remove them from the cooker, but don't worry – they'll still taste very good.)

Cider ribs
Serves 1

8 oz (200 g) spare ribs or chicken drumsticks
1 tablespoon (15 ml) honey
1 tablespoon (15 ml) vinegar
1 tablespoon (15 ml) soy sauce
1 tablespoon (15 ml) tomato purée
3 fl oz (75 ml) cider
mixed herbs
7 oz (175 g) sweetcorn

Heat the empty slow-cooker for 10 minutes. In a small pan gently heat all the ingredients apart from the meat. Then place the meat in the pre-warmed cooker and pour the sauce over. Cook for 7–9 hours, Serve with rice or potatoes. If you prefer your ribs crispy put them under a hot grill while you are cooking the rice or potatoes.

Rats-in-a-pot

Serves 1

1 aubergine, sliced
1 small onion, sliced
8 oz (200 g) courgettes, sliced
1 small green pepper, sliced
7-oz (175-g) can tomatoes, roughly chopped
1 clove garlic, crushed or chopped
mixed herbs
2 oz (50 g) grated cheese

Put everything except the cheese into the slow-cooker. Cook for 8-10 hours. Serve with some rice and the cheese on top.

Saucy cabbage rolls

Serves 1

3 savoy or celtic-type cabbage leaves
1 small onion, finely chopped
4 oz (100 g) lean minced beef
1 teaspoon (5 ml) mixed herbs
1 tablespoon (15 ml) brown sugar
8-oz (200-g) can tomatoes, roughly chopped
1 tablespoon (15 ml) tomato and vegetable soup mix from a packet soup

Wash the cabbage, then boil in water for 1 minute. Drain. Mix the onion, mince and herbs together. Divide this mixture between the leaves, placing the filling at the stalk ends. Fold the leaf sides inwards and then roll up the leaf. Place the rolls, with the leaf join underneath, in the slow-cooker. Cover with the sugar and then with the tomatoes. Cook for 6-8 hours. When cooked, remove the rolls from the cooker, tip the juices into a small pan and heat up with the soup mixture, simmer until thickened and pour over the rolls. Serve with rice.

Spicy sausages
Serves 1

    7-oz (175-g) can chilli beans
    4-6 oz (100-150 g) chipolata sausages
    7-oz (175-g) can tomatoes, roughly chopped
    1 small onion, chopped
    1 small green pepper, chopped
    1 teaspoon (5 ml) paprika
    couple dashes worcester sauce
    1 tablespoon (15 ml) tomato purée

Put all the ingredients into the slow-cooker. Cook for 6-8 hours.
Serve with potato and a vegetable.

Barbecue pot
Serves 1

    12 oz (300 g) fresh vegetables, peeled and chopped
    1 small onion, chopped
    7 oz (175 g) canned kidney beans
    7 oz (175 g) canned baked beans
    1 tablespoon (15 ml) honey
    1 tablespoon (15 ml) soy sauce
    1 tablespoon (15 ml) tomato purée
    chilli powder to taste
    1 teaspoon (5 ml) mustard (optional)
    1 tablespoon (15 ml) vinegar
    a little orange juice
    5 fl oz (125 ml) hot stock

Put all the ingredients into the slow-cooker. Cook for 8-10 hours.
Serve with rice.

Mushroom-stuffed peppers

Serves 1

  1 medium green pepper
  1 small onion, finely chopped
  2 oz (50 g) mushrooms, finely chopped
  1 oz (25 g) grated cheese
  1 tablespoon (15 ml) milk
  Italian seasoning
  7-oz (175-g) can tomatoes, roughly chopped
  1 tablespoon (15 ml) tomato and vegetable soup mix from a
    packet soup

Cut the top off the pepper and remove the seeds. Mix the onion, mushroom, cheese, milk and seasoning together. Use this to stuff the pepper. Put into the slow-cooker with the tomatoes. Cook for 5-7 hours. When cooked, remove the pepper, tip the juices into a small pan, add the soup mixture and simmer until thick. Pour over the pepper and serve with pasta or potatoes.

Fish stew

Serves 1

  8 oz (200 g) white fish fillet
  8 oz (200 g) courgette or carrot, sliced
  1 small onion, chopped
  7-oz (175-g) can tomatoes, roughly chopped
  1 tablespoon (15 ml) tomato purée
  1 clove garlic, crushed or chopped
  mixed herbs

Cut the fish fillet into cubes, put all the ingredients into the slow-cooker and mix well. Cook for 4-6 hours. Serve with rice.

Tasty tuna

Serves 1

    5 oz (125 g) condensed tomato soup
    7 oz (175 g) sweetcorn
    3-oz (100-g) can tuna, drained
    Italian seasoning
    3 pieces pre-cooked lasagne
    1 oz (25 g) grated cheese mixed with 1 tablespoon (15 ml)
        natural yoghurt

Put one-third of the soup into the slow-cooker. Mix the sweet-corn, tuna and seasoning together. Put one slice of lasagne into the cooker; cover with half the tuna mixture. Put another slice of lasagne on the mixture, cover with another third of the soup and then the rest of the tuna mixture. Cover with the rest of the soup and then with the cheese and yoghurt mixture. Cook for 4-6 hours. Serve with salad.

Dark beans

Serves 1

    7-oz (175-g) can chilli beans
    7 oz (175 g) canned kidney beans
    7-oz (175-g) can tomatoes, roughly chopped
    1 small onion, chopped
    1 small green pepper, chopped
    1 tablespoon (15 ml) dark brown sugar
    1 tablespoon (15 ml) black treacle

Put all the ingredients into the slow cooker. Cook for 6-8 hours. Serve with rice.

Chicken à la Cas

Serves 1

  8 oz (200 g) chicken portion, with skin removed
  1 small onion, chopped
  1 small green pepper, chopped
  2 oz (50 g) mushrooms, chopped
  3 fl oz (75 ml) chicken stock or wine
  1 tablespoon (15 ml) tomato purée
  1 clove garlic, crushed or chopped
  mixed herbs
  1 tablespoon (15 ml) flour

Put all the ingredients apart from the flour into the slow-cooker. Cook for 7-9 hours. Thirty minutes before serving blend the flour with a little water and add to the cooker to thicken the sauce. Serve with rice or potatoes and a green vegetable.

Korma curry

Serves 1

  8 oz (200 g) lamb, boned and cubed *or* 8 oz (200 g) root
    vegetables, peeled and cubed
  1 small onion, cut into eight pieces
  1 tablespoon (15 ml) tomato purée
  sprinkling ginger
  chilli to taste
  1 teaspoon (5 ml) curry powder
  7 fl oz (175 ml) chicken or vegetable stock
  1 teaspoon (5 ml) curry powder
  7 fl oz (175 ml) chicken or vegetable stock
  1 tablespoon (15 ml) flour
  1 tablespoon (15 ml) natural yoghurt

Put all the ingredients apart from the flour and yoghurt into the cooker. Cook for 7-9 hours. Thirty minutes before serving blend the flour with a little water and add to the cooker. To serve, mix in the yoghurt and serve on a bed of rice.

Creole casserole

Serves 1

7-oz (175-g) can chilli beans
7-oz (175-g) can tomatoes, roughly chopped
1 small onion, chopped
1 small green pepper, chopped
1 clove garlic, crushed or chopped

Put all the ingredients into the slow-cooker. Cook for 7-9 hours. Serve with rice.

Pork and parsnips

Serves 1

8 oz (200 g) parsnips, peeled and cut into small chunks
8 oz (200 g) pork (a chop or lean fillet)
1 medium potato, peeled and cut into small chunks
1 small onion, chopped
1 tablespoon (15 ml) peanut butter
7 fl oz (175 ml) hot white stock
1 tablespoon (15 ml) grated coconut
1 tablespoon (15 ml) flour

Dissolve the peanut butter in the hot stock, then put all ingredients apart from the flour into the slow-cooker. Cook for 7-9 hours. Thirty minutes before serving blend the flour with a little water and add to the cooker. Serve with rice or pasta.

Bolognese risotto

Serves 1

4 oz (100 g) minced beef
1 small green pepper, chopped
1 small onion, chopped
2 oz (50 g) mushrooms, chopped
7-oz (175-g) can tomatoes, roughly chopped
Italian seasoning
2 oz (50 g) easy-cook long-grain rice
5 fl oz (125 ml) hot beef stock

Put all the ingredients into the slow-cooker. Stir well. Cook for 4-5 hours. Serve with parmesan cheese.

12 Teach Yourself Italian

Italian food has been a great favourite with students for many years, and is now more popular than ever. Perhaps this is because it is genuinely foolproof, everyone likes it and the ingredients are both cheap and universally available. This chapter shows you yet more wonderful ways of cooking the two most famous Italian foods, pasta and pizza, and also introduces you to some less familiar but no less delicious dishes.

I should like to dispel the long-standing myth that Italian food is bad for you. True, pasta can be fattening if eaten in large quantities, but it can form the basis of a healthy diet if, like the Italians, you balance it with fresh vegetables and meat and go easy on the creamy/buttery sauces.

Pasta is the perfect standby for anyone on a budget, or with restricted cooking facilities: it is quick to cook, cheap, doesn't go off and can make a nourishing, tasty meal. There are numerous varieties on the market, including fresh pasta, now available in a great many supermarkets, so it is easy to be adventurous.

I've included two types of pizza in this chapter. One is the real thing, just like Mamma used to make, and is for those of you who actually enjoy spending hours preparing food that will be devoured in a flash by admiring friends. The other version can be made in a frying-pan in a matter of minutes, and is designed for the average person who loves the taste of fresh pizza but is too lazy (or hungry) to wait.

The Italians are creative cooks, and this can best be seen in their imaginative ways with vegetables. Many of the recipes in this chapter are meatless, but they will appeal to vegetarians and meat-eaters alike. The first recipe is a good example of the Italian gift for turning a rather mundane vegetable into a mouthwatering dish.

One of the reasons for the large quantities of Italian-inspired food consumed by students is that it can be very cheap indeed, as well as very filling. Its staple ingredients – pasta, rice, flour – do not cost much and they can be combined with vegetables, cheese or cheap cuts of meat to make an economical meal.

Spaghetti bolognese has a place in all our hearts, but this chapter will show you how much more there is to teaching yourself Italian.

Buon appetito!

Rice-stuffed courgettes
Serves 2

    1 tablespoon (15 ml) oil
    1 onion, chopped
    1 clove garlic, crushed or chopped
    8-oz (200-g) can tomatoes
    1 tablespoon (15 ml) tomato purée
    2 teaspoons (10 ml) Italian seasoning
·   2 large courgettes
    4 oz (100 g) cottage cheese
    4 tablespoons (60 ml) cooked brown rice
    2 oz (50 g) cheese, grated

Fry the onion and garlic in the oil. When soft add the tomatoes and tomato purée. Stir in the herbs and then simmer for 15 minutes until you have a thick sauce. Meanwhile cut the courgettes in half, scoop out the middles and discard. Mix the cottage cheese and rice and use this mixture to stuff the courgettes. Put a layer of the sauce in a casserole dish, then place the courgettes on top. Cover with the grated cheese and bake in a pre-heated oven at 200°C/400°F/Gas 6 for 20-25 minutes until brown. Serve with the rest of the sauce and a salad or green vegetables.

Pasta carbonara
Serves 2

    4 oz (100 g) pasta
    1 tablespoon (15 ml) oil
    2 ham steaks, chopped
    1 egg, beaten
    2 oz (50 g) cheese, finely grated

Cook the pasta in boiling water for 8-10 minutes. Heat the oil and add the ham and cooked pasta, followed by the egg and the cheese. Mix well and serve immediately (the heat of the pasta and oil cooks the egg). This is good with some crusty bread and either a green vegetable or a salad.

Risotto bolognese
Serves 2

- 1 tablespoon (15 ml) oil
- 1 onion, chopped
- 2 cloves garlic, crushed or chopped
- 8 oz (200 g) minced meat
- 2 bacon steaks, chopped
- 2 tablespoons (30 ml) tomato purée
- 2 teaspoons (10 ml) Italian seasoning
- 8 fl oz (200 ml) water
- 1 tablespoon (15 ml) butter
- 8 oz (200 g) Italian risotto rice
- 1 pint (500 ml) hot brown stock
- 2 tablespoons (30 ml) Parmesan cheese

Fry the onion and garlic in the oil until soft. Add the mince and cook until browned. Stir in the bacon, tomato purée, Italian seasoning and water. Simmer gently for 15-20 minutes. Meanwhile cook the rice. Melt the butter in a medium-sized saucepan, add the rice and stir until it becomes transparent. Pour in one-third of the stock and cook until the liquid is absorbed; add another third and again cook until the liquid is absorbed. Add the last of the stock and cook until just absorbed. Stir together the meat sauce and rice, heat through and then serve with the Parmesan cheese sprinkled on top.

Vegetarian risotto with peanut sauce
Serves 2

> 1 tablespoon (15 ml) oil
> 1 onion, chopped
> 1 clove garlic, crushed or chopped
> 4 oz (100 g) mushrooms, quartered
> 8 oz (200 g) brown rice
> 1 pint (500 ml) vegetable stock
> 1 banana, chopped
> 2 oz (50 g) peanuts
> 2 tablespoons (30 ml) crunchy peanut butter
> 1 teaspoon (5 ml) paprika
> 3 tablespoons (45 ml) water

Fry the onion, garlic and mushrooms in oil until soft. Add the rice and one-third of the stock. Cook until the liquid is absorbed, then add another third of the stock. When that is absorbed, add the last of the stock and stir in the banana and peanuts. Blend the peanut butter with the paprika and water to make the sauce, and when the last of the stock has been absorbed serve the risotto with the sauce.

Cod with onion sauce
Serves 2

> 2 cod fillets in crispy breadcrumbs
> 1 onion, chopped
> 1 clove garlic, chopped or crushed
> 1 tablespoon (15 ml) oil
> 6 fl oz (150 ml) hot beef stock
> 1 tablespoon (15 ml) tomato purée
> pinch mixed herbs
> 1 tablespoon (15 ml) cornflour

Grill the cod fillets for 15 minutes, turning frequently. Fry the onion and garlic in oil until soft. Add the stock, tomato purée and herbs. Bring to the boil, cover and simmer for 10 minutes. Blend the cornflour with a little water, add to the sauce and stir until it thickens. Serve the cod fillets with the sauce and vegetables.

Spinach and cheese pancakes
Serves 2

3 oz (75 g) wholemeal flour
1 egg, beaten
10 fl oz (250 ml) milk
oil for frying
2 lb (800 g) spinach, coarse stems removed
8 oz (200 g) cottage cheese
Sauce
1 oz (25 g) butter
1 oz (25 g) wholemeal flour
8 fl oz (200 ml) milk
2 oz (50 g) grated cheese
salt and pepper

Put the flour in a mixing bowl. Make a well in the middle and put the egg into this. Start to beat the egg into the flour with a fork while gradually adding the milk. Beat until the batter is smooth. Heat a little oil in a frying-pan. Add some batter to the pan and swirl to coat the base. Cook for 1-2 minutes. Flip over and cook for 1 minute. Make 8 pancakes and keep them warm. Chop and then wash the spinach, leaving water clinging to the leaves. Cook in a covered saucepan for 4 minutes. Mix the spinach with the cottage cheese and season to taste. Divide the mixture between the pancakes and roll each of them up. Place in a greased casserole dish.

To make the sauce, melt the butter, then take off the heat and add the flour. Mix well and gradually add the milk. Return to the heat and stir until the sauce thickens. Add the grated cheese. Season. Cover the pancakes with the sauce and bake in a pre-heated oven at 180°C/350°F/Gas 4 for 35 minutes. Serve with a salad.

Stuffed peppers in tomato sauce
Serves 2

>   2 green peppers
>   1 onion, chopped
>   1 clove garlic, crushed or chopped
>   1 tablespoon (15 ml) oil
>   8 oz (200 g) minced meat
>   2 tablespoons (30 ml) tomato purée
>   4 tablespoons (60 ml) hot beef stock
>   14-oz (200-g) can tomatoes
>   1 tablespoon (15 ml) cornflour

Cut the stalk end off the peppers and retain. Scoop out the seeds. Fry the onion and garlic in oil until soft. Add the mince and cook until brown. Stir in the tomato purée, stock and herbs. Simmer for 10 minutes.

To make the tomato sauce, drain the juice from the can into a small saucepan. Roughly chop the tomatoes, add to the juice, and heat gently. Blend the cornflour with a little water and add to the saucepan. Stir until the mixture thickens. Put a layer of the sauce into a casserole dish and place the peppers on top. Stuff the peppers with the mince mixture, replace the stalk end and cover with sauce. Bake in a pre-heated oven at 190°C/375°F/Gas 5 for 30 minutes. Serve with rice.

Pasta with mushroom sauce
Serves 2

>   4 oz (100 g) pasta
>   1 onion, sliced
>   2 cloves garlic, crushed and chopped
>   4 oz (100 g) mushrooms, sliced
>   1 tablespoon (15 ml) oil
>   2 teaspoons (10 ml) tomato purée
>   2 teaspoons (10 ml) soy sauce
>   1 teaspoon (5 ml) Italian seasoning
>   5-oz (125-ml) can condensed mushroom soup

Cook the pasta for 10 minutes or as directed on the packet. Make the sauce by frying the onion, garlic and mushrooms in the oil. Add the rest of the ingredients and heat through until bubbling. Serve the pasta with the sauce poured over it.

Crusted mince
Serves 2

> 1 onion, sliced
> 1 clove garlic, crushed or chopped
> 1 tablespoon (15 ml) oil
> 8 oz (200 g) minced meat
> 15 fl oz (375 ml) hot beef stock
> 1 tablespoon (15 ml) tomato purée
> 2 teaspoons (10 ml) mixed herbs
> dash worcester sauce
> 2 teaspoons (10 ml) cornflour
> 4 slices french bread
> oil for frying

Fry the onion and garlic in oil until soft. Add the mince and cook until brown. Stir in the stock, tomato purée, herbs and worcester sauce. Simmer for 10 minutes. Blend the cornflour with a little water, add to the mince mixture and cook until it thickens. Pour the mixture into a casserole dish. Pour a little oil into the same frying-pan and very quickly brown the bread on both sides. Take each bread slice and push into the gravy, then turn and lay it in the mixture. Cook in a pre-heated oven at 170°C/325°F/Gas 3 for 30-40 minutes until the top is crisp. Serve with a baked potato and a green vegetable.

Vegetable and pasta soup
Serves 2

> 16-oz (400-g) can chopped tomatoes
> 8-oz (200-g) can any cooked beans
> 6 fl oz (150 ml) hot vegetable stock
> 1 clove garlic, crushed or chopped
> 1 teaspoon (5 ml) Italian seasoning
> 2 oz (50 g) quick-cook macaroni or cooked pasta
> 4 oz (100 g) frozen peas or sweetcorn

Put all the ingredients in a saucepan. Bring to the boil and then simmer for 20-25 minutes. Serve with crusty bread and grated cheese.

Leek and courgette gratin
Serves 2

1 large courgette, sliced
12 oz (300 g) leeks, sliced
2 tablespoons (30 ml) oil
1 oz (25 g) butter
1 oz (25 g) flour
10 fl oz (250 ml) milk
4 oz (100 g) cheese, grated
2 cloves garlic, crushed or chopped
4 slices french bread
oil for frying

Fry the courgettes and leeks in oil until soft, then put them into a greased casserole dish. Make a sauce by melting the butter and then taking the pan off the heat, adding the flour and mixing well. Gradually add the milk and then return the pan to the heat and stir until the mixture thickens. Add half the cheese and mix well. Pour the sauce over the vegetables. Heat the oil and gently fry the garlic. Add the bread slices and quickly fry on both sides. Place the bread in the casserole and scatter the remaining cheese over the top. Cook in a pre-heated oven at 200°C/400°F/Gas 6 for 30 minutes or until golden in colour.

Pan pizza
Serves 2

> 6 oz (150 g) self-raising flour
> 1 teaspoon (5 ml) salt
> 4 teaspoons (20 ml) oil
> oil for frying
> 2 tablespoons (30 ml) tomato purée
> 8-oz (200-g) can tomatoes, drained and roughly chopped
> 1 teaspoon (5 ml) Italian seasoning
> 4-oz (100-g) can sardines in oil, drained
> 2 oz (50 g) cheese, grated

Mix the flour, salt and oil together. Add enough water (approximately 6 tablespoons/90 ml) to make a soft dough. Knead for a few minutes, then press out to fill a large frying-pan. Fry for 4 minutes, then turn it over and fry the other side. Spread with the purée and herbs, then top with the tomatoes and sardines. Scatter the cheese on top and grill until the cheese has melted and is bubbling. Serve with salad.

Frittata
Serves 2

> oil for frying
> ½ red pepper, chopped
> 3 eggs, beaten
> 8-oz (200-g) can sweetcorn
> 2 tablespoons (30 ml) milk
> 2 oz (50 g) cheese, grated
> salt and pepper

Fry the pepper while you are mixing the other ingredients together. Pour these into a frying-pan and mix with the peppers. Cook for 5 minutes and then for a further 5 minutes under the grill. (If you have a deft wrist you can turn the omelette over and fry both sides.)

Pasta frittata
Serves 2

oil for frying
4 eggs, beaten
2 oz (50 g) cooked pasta
4-oz (100-g) can tuna, drained
2 oz (50 g) cheese, grated
1 tablespoon (15 ml) milk
1 tablespoon (15 ml) tomato sauce
dash of worcester sauce

Mix all the ingredients together and pour into some heated oil.
Fry for 5 minutes and then grill for 5 minutes.

Pizza
Serves 2-3

1 teaspoon (5 ml) brown sugar
5 fl oz (125 ml) tepid water
1 teaspoon (5 ml) dried yeast
4 oz (100 g) strong wholemeal flour
4 oz (100 g) self-raising wholemeal flour
1 teaspoon (5 ml) salt
1 teaspoon (5 ml) oil
16-oz (400-g) can chopped tomatoes
1 tablespoon (15 ml) tomato purée
1 teaspoon (5 ml) Italian seasoning
1 onion, chopped and fried in butter
3 oz (75 g) cheese, preferably mozzarella
3 tablespoons (45 ml) Parmesan cheese

Dissolve the sugar in the water and sprinkle with the yeast. Leave
in a warm place for 10-15 minutes or until frothy. Sift the flour
and salt in a bowl and add the yeast mixture and oil. Knead for 5
minutes. Put in a floured bowl and cover with a damp tea-towel,
then put in a warm place and leave for 30 minutes. Bring the
tomatoes, tomato purée and herbs to the boil and simmer for
15-20 minutes until thick. Knead the dough again and roll out to
a 10-inch (25-cm) round. Place on a greased baking tray. Cover
with the tomato mixture. Layer with the onions and slices of
mozzarella or grated cheese. Sprinkle the Parmesan on top. Bake
in a pre-heated oven at 200°C/400°F/Gas 6 for 30 minutes. Serve
with a salad.

Baked pasta
Serves 2

- 4 oz (100 g) cooked pasta
- 8 oz (200 g) minced meat
- 1 onion, finely chopped
- 2 tablespoons (30 ml) oil
- 2 tablespoons (30 ml) tomato purée
- 2 teaspoons (10 ml) Italian seasoning
- 1 clove garlic, crushed or chopped
- 15 fl oz (375 ml) hot beef stock
- 1 oz (25 g) butter
- 1 oz (25 g) wholemeal flour
- 6 fl oz (150 ml) milk
- 2 oz (50 g) cheese, grated
- 1 oz (25 g) breadcrumbs
- 2 tablespoons (30 ml) Parmesan cheese

Fry the mince and onion in oil until brown. Add the tomato purée, herbs, garlic and stock and stir well. Simmer for 5-10 minutes until most of the liquid is absorbed. Mix with the pasta and put in a greased casserole dish. Make a cheese sauce by melting the butter, taking the pan off the heat and adding the flour. Mix well and gradually add the milk; return to the heat and stir until the mixture thickens. Add the cheese and spoon over the meat mixture. Mix the Parmesan and breadcrumbs and scatter on top of the casserole. Bake in a pre-heated oven at 180°C/375°F/Gas 5 for 30-40 minutes until brown and crisp on top. Serve with a green vegetable and a baked potato.

Mushroom-stuffed pasta
Serves 2

8 oz (200 g) strong wholemeal flour
2 eggs
8 oz (200 g) mushrooms, finely chopped
½ onion, finely chopped
2 oz (50 g) butter
1 clove garlic, crushed or chopped
1 teaspoon (5 ml) Italian seasoning
1 tablespoon (15 ml) tomato purée
5-oz (125-g) can condensed mushroom soup
1 tablespoon (15 ml) red wine

Put the flour on a clean, smooth surface and make a well in the middle. Break the eggs into this and, using a knife, gradually mix the two together. When mixed, knead for 10 minutes. Leave under a bowl for 30 minutes.

Fry the mushrooms and onions in the butter. When most of the butter has evaporated, add the garlic, herbs and tomato purée. Mix well and cook until all the liquid has been absorbed. Put aside to use as stuffing.

Knead the dough again and divide into two balls. Put one under the bowl while rolling the other out to a 10-inch (25-cm) round. Straighten the ends and divide into 12 squares. Put a little of the stuffing into each square and fold into a triangle. Press the sides firmly together and then turn two corners back and press together so you have a little hat. Put these on a plate and cover with a damp tea-towel. Now do the same with the other half of the dough.

Bring a large saucepan of water to the boil. Cook six of the little hats at a time, removing them from the pot as they rise to the surface. To make a sauce to serve with them, add the condensed soup and the wine to the leftover stuffing and warm it through.

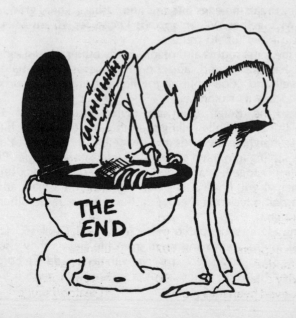

Index

TISH HAYTON
THE FOOD ADDICT'S DIET

**The new, fail-safe way
to control your appetite,
lose weight and eat well**

Are you overweight? Do you break every new diet you go on? Do you often feel tired or under the weather?

This revolutionary book shows you how overweight, lack of appetite control and a hoard of minor ailments can all be linked to one thing — an addiction to food. But food addiction is not a sign of personal weakness — you have much more will power than you think — and, what's more, it is curable.

By following the Food Addict's Diet and eliminating the four main culprits for just three weeks, but eating *unlimited quantities* of nearly 200 other delicious foods, you will not only learn how to lose weight and stay slim by controlling your desires for fattening foods, but you will also gain a whole new lease of life.

★ Mouth-watering recipes

★ Revealing self-help questionnaires

★ Inspiring case histories

'I am never starving hungry and I never feel like bingeing now. I can't thank you enough for introducing me to this healthier way of eating' — Mrs J.F., St Albans

NON-FICTION/HEALTH   0 7472 3476 0

──BARBARA KAFKA──
MICROWAVE GOURMET
THE DEFINITIVE MICROWAVE COOKBOOK

'An extraordinary, comprehensive book'
Jane Grigson, *Observer*

What do you use *your* microwave for?

To warm up coffee? Defrost bread from the freezer? Heat up
ready-prepared supermarket meals? Bake a potato or two?

Yes, but what else can it do?

In this definitive guide to microwave cooking, Barbara Kafka
shows, with a dazzling combination of culinary flair and
scientific exactitude, how, by using a little care and
imagination, you can make delicious meals out of fresh
ingredients quickly and efficiently.

With over 600 recipes, a comprehensive dictionary of foods
and techniques and advice on what the microwave can and
cannot do, *Microwave Gourmet* covers everything from such
basics as vegetable stock through classic dishes like Moules
Marinières to rich dinner-party fare. Using precise easy-to-
follow instructions, Barbara Kafka explains how to cook
Paupiettes of Sole Stuffed with Salmon in three minutes,
plum jam in thirteen minutes and artichokes in seven. As she
herself says, 'It may not be a mystic experience, but it sure is
quick and efficient.' Whether you are a beginner or an
experienced microwave cook, *Microwave Gourmet* will prove
to be as indispensable as your microwave itself.

'I feel fairly certain that it will make all other books on
microwave cookery redundant' Paul Levy, *Observer*

'This intelligent person's guide to the microwave . . . is long
overdue' *Sunday Times*

'The book I've turned to again and again has been Barbara
Kafka's *Microwave Gourmet*' Sophie Grigson,
Evening Standard

'This stupendously good book' *Cosmopolitan*

NON-FICTION/COOKERY   0 7472 3380 2

A selection of bestsellers
from Headline

FICTION

THE FIFTH PROFESSION	David Morrell	£4.99 □
TABLES	John Lucas	£4.99 □
ENTICEMENTS	Una-Mary Parker	£4.99 □
OUR FAMILY	Victor Pemberton	£4.50 □
FORTUNE	Ritchie Smith	£4.99 □
ADVENTURELAND	Steve Harris	£4.99 □
PASSION NEVER KNOWS	Adam Kennedy	£4.99 □
ARMY BLUE	Lucian K Truscott IV	£4.99 □

NON-FICTION

TOM JONES: A Biography	Stafford Hildred & David Gritten	£3.99 □
THE FOOD ADDICT'S DIET	Tish Hayton	£3.99 □

SCIENCE FICTION AND FANTASY

THE HOUSE OF CTHULHU Tales from The Primal Land Volume Two	Brian Lumley	£3.99 □
TALIESIN'S TELLING Daughter of Tintagel 4	Fay Sampson	£3.99 □
THE CRYSTAL KEEP	Sheila Gilluly	£4.99 □

All Headline books are available at your local bookshop or newsagent, or can be ordered direct from the publisher. Just tick the titles you want and fill in the form below. Prices and availability subject to change without notice.

Headline Book Publishing PLC, Cash Sales Department, PO Box 11, Falmouth, Cornwall, TR10 9EN, England.

Please enclose a cheque or postal order to the value of the cover price and allow the following for postage and packing:
UK: 80p for the first book and 20p for each additional book ordered up to a maximum charge of £2.00
BFPO: 80p for the first book and 20p for each additional book
OVERSEAS & EIRE: £1.50 for the first book, £1.00 for the second book and 30p for each subsequent book.

Name ....

Address ....

....

....